DECEMBER 2025

SUN	MON	TUE	WED	THU	FRI	SAT
	1	2	3	4	5	6
7	8	9	10	11	12	13
14	15	16	17	18	19	20
21	22	23	24	25	26	27
28	29	30	31			

Dear Child Care Professional,

Thanks for choosing the *2026 Redleaf Calendar-Keeper*!

As in years past, this edition of the *Redleaf Calendar-Keeper* contains all the trusted worksheets, expense charts, and tools you rely on to maintain accurate and detailed business records throughout the year. The more information you capture in your *Redleaf Calendar-Keeper*, the more money and time you will save on your taxes.

In addition to all of the record-keeping benefits, a number of great features and items of note are included in this year's *Redleaf Calendar-Keeper*.

Antiracist Themes, Children's Books, and Activities for Young Children

The more opportunities children have to see and share experiences with people of diverse races (including through books like *Who's in My Family?*, *All About Families*, and *All the Colors We Are*), the less preference they show toward their own race. Along with recommended children's books, throughout the *2026 Redleaf Calendar-Keeper* you will find antiracist activities for children you can easily incorporate into your day. It is never too early to start teaching the value of diversity.

Up-to-Date USDA Reimbursement Guidelines

Every year we research for updates to the United States Department of Agriculture's (USDA's) Child and Adult Care Food Program (CACFP) and integrate any new information so you won't have to worry about identifying the new regulations yourself. Still unsure of ounce equivalents? Go to the Calendar-Keeper web page or RedleafPress.org for easy-to-understand charts.

Literacy Corner

Literacy development starts early in life and is important in developing cognitive skills. The educational and emotional benefits of reading together prepare young children to succeed in school. Each month you will find two suggested children's books that correspond with the month's theme. Many of the 24 children's books, including *All the Colors We Are/Todos los colores de nuestra piel* by Katie Kissinger and *When You Just Have to Roar!* by Rachel Robertson, are available at RedleafPress.org/Childrens-Books.

Activities for Children

Ninety percent of brain development occurs by the time a child is five years old. That means those early years are really important! All the inspiration and activities featured in this year's Calendar-Keeper are from Redleaf Press books, including *I Like Myself: Fostering Positive Racial Identity in Young Black Children* by Toni Sturdivant and *Teaching STEM in the Early Years: Activities for Integrating Science, Technology, Engineering, and Mathematics*, 2nd edition, by Sally Moomaw. Use these ideas to promote healthy brain development and social-emotional learning in the children you care for.

The Experienced Provider

As a child care provider, you have to address many challenges throughout the day. This year's Calendar-Keeper has advice from a variety of Redleaf Press resources, including *Loose Parts in Action: The Essential How-To Guide* by Lisa Daly. The new third edition of *The Redleaf Family Child Care Curriculum: Teaching Through Quality Care* by Sharon Woodward, revised by Bisa Batten Lewis EdD, is featured widely throughout.

Have a wonderful year!

Your friends at Redleaf Press

The Think Small Institute

Think Small and Redleaf Press have been advancing quality care and education for young children for over fifty years. A lot has changed since opening our doors in 1971, but what remains constant is our drive to find innovative ways to support families, early childhood professionals, policy-makers, and other influential people in making the best choices for children.

Our latest innovative solution is the Think Small Institute, which aims to transform how you access resources you need for the children in your care. And these online training courses are just the beginning. We are working hard to build a virtual hub to meet all your professional development needs by offering:

- Premium, On-Demand Courses
- In-Depth, Live, Instructor-Led Trainings
- Tailored Trainings
- Facilitated Communities of Practice

Thinksmall.org/shop

Redleaf Press Family Child Care Resources

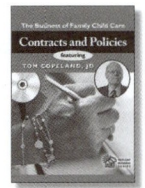

The Business of Family Child Care: Contracts and Policies
Most family child care providers would rather care for children than write and enforce contracts and policies, but taking care of the children is only part of the job. Contracts and policies are another important part of running a business. This video can help you understand how to establish a good business relationship with the families you serve by creating clear contracts and policies and enforcing them fairly.

#548029-CK26 $29.95

The Business of Family Child Care: Record-Keeping
Most family child care providers would rather care for children than spend time keeping records. But record keeping is an important part of running a business. This training video can help you understand proper record-keeping strategies, help lower taxes, and save family child care providers money.

#547329-CK26 $49.95

The Redleaf Complete Forms Kit
For Both Family Child Care and Center-Based Programs, Revised Edition

Keep your business organized and save hours of time! This CD-ROM includes more than 150 child care forms—the most comprehensive and professionally presented forms available. CD-ROM.

#546520-CK26 $24.95

Infant Daily Report or Toddler Daily Report
Parents fill out the top half of these handy sheets at drop-off, and you report diapering, feeding, napping, and eating information on the bottom half. You'll receive three tablets, each with 60 pages—a six-month supply.

#112101-CK26 $14.95   **#112701-CK26** $12.95

Daily Lesson Planner
Schedule your day with this planning aid. It has space to conveniently keep track of activities, learning centers, and more. The planner is on a six-day-per-week cycle. You'll receive three tablets, which are three-hole punched, each with 60 pages—a six-month supply.

#112501-CK26 $14.95

Injury Log
Document injuries on these weekly sheets. Each form is organized with areas to record all relevant information. The tablet is three-hole punched and has 55 forms.

#112301-CK26 $9.95

The Redleaf Family Child Care Curriculum Complete Set
Sharon Woodward

Save over $20 when you buy the set!

#548587-CK26 $59.95

This starter set includes:

The Redleaf Family Child Care Curriculum, 3rd Edition
Provide high-quality care with this easy-to-use complete curriculum designed for family child care programs with mixed-age children. 272 pgs.

#548586-CK26 $44.95

The Redleaf Family Child Care Curriculum Developmental Assessment, Third Edition (10 copies)
Observe and record a child's growth and development with the *Developmental Assessment*.

#548777-CK26 $16.95

The Redleaf Family Child Care Curriculum Family Companion, Third Edition (10 Copies)
Give families an overview of the *Family Child Care Curriculum*.

#548784-CK26 $12.95

The Redleaf Family Child Care Curriculum Developmental Assessment Guide, Third Edition
This guide walks you through the process of using the *Developmental Assessment* tool and provides tips to help you communicate with families.

#548791-CK26 $9.95

> *The Redleaf Family Child Care Curriculum* and supplemental materials are available in Spanish! Visit RedleafPress.org for more information (#547177-CK26)

Family Child Care Homes
Creative Spaces for Children to Learn
Linda J. Armstrong

Create warm and inviting places where children feel at home. Loaded with photographs of inventive and practical spaces, you will find inspiration to create your own stimulating and cozy environment. Softbound, 216 pgs.

#540757-CK26 $49.95

Protecting Your Family Child Care Business
Preventing and Addressing Regulatory Challenges
Sharon Woodward

Protect your family child care business—your livelihood and the heart of your home from citations, allegations, and infractions. Softbound, 144 pgs.

#548371-CK26 $21.95

Save Time and Money Using the *Redleaf Calendar-Keeper*

For 49 years, the *Redleaf Calendar-Keeper* has saved countless hours of record keeping for family child care providers across the country. It has also helped hundreds of thousands of providers to significantly reduce their taxes.

2026

The *Redleaf Calendar-Keeper* is part of a series of record-keeping resources from Redleaf Press that include the following titles:

- *Family Child Care Record-Keeping Guide, 9th edition*: Identifies over 1,000 business deductions
- *Family Child Care Tax Workbook and Organizer*: Use it to do your own taxes
- *Family Child Care Tax Companion*: Use it to educate your tax professional

With these resources, you can keep accurate and detailed records that may mean big tax savings. Here are some important tips for using the *Redleaf Calendar-Keeper* most efficiently.

Three Key Record-Keeping Rules

1. Save receipts for all expenses associated with cleaning, repairing, and maintaining your home.
2. Record all meals served to the children in your care on a daily basis, including all meals not reimbursed by the Food Program.
3. For at least two months, track all the hours you use your home for business, particularly the hours you spend cleaning, preparing activities, and doing other business-related tasks when the children are not present.

How the *Redleaf Calendar-Keeper* Makes Filing Taxes Easier

Virtually all providers must file IRS Form 1040 Schedule C. It is easier to complete the Schedule C when you keep track of your expenses on the *Redleaf Calendar-Keeper*, which uses the same categories that appear on the Schedule C. In fact, the expenses on the monthly expense report pages are listed in the exact order that they appear on the Schedule C. In addition, we have included five expense categories at the end of the second monthly expense report page: food, toys, household items, cleaning supplies, and activity expenses. These expense categories do not appear directly on the Schedule C, but we've created them to make it easier for you to enter your expenses on the Schedule C. We recommend that you use the series of blank lines under "Other Expenses" on the back of the Schedule C as a place to record these expense categories or other expense categories you have created.

It is important to understand that business expenses can be recorded under any category. For example, children's birthday cards can be recorded under supplies or activity expenses. You can cross out some categories listed in the *Redleaf Calendar-Keeper* and customize the categories for your own use. We left space on these pages to rename a category or to add more categories. In the end, all of your expenses will be totaled on the Schedule C, so you do not need to worry about the placement of an expense in a particular category.

To make it easier to enter expenses under the categories on the *Redleaf Calendar-Keeper* and the Schedule C, we have identified more than one thousand allowable deductions and their expense categories in the *Family Child Care Record-Keeping Guide*, 9th edition, by Tom Copeland, available from Redleaf Press.

How to Track 100% Business Expenses

It is important that you identify which items are used 100% for business because they are worth more in deductions than items partially used for business. Individual items used 100% for business should be identified as such on the receipt. There are several ways items can be entered in the *Redleaf Calendar-Keeper*. You can write "100%" next to the expense when entering it on the monthly expense report. The 100% items should be added up separately at the end of the year. A Time-Space percentage should be used on all other items in each expense category. For example, let's say you have six items of supplies used 100% for business, totaling $200. Another 25 supply items are used both for business and for your family, totaling $1,000. If your Time-Space percentage is 40%, you can deduct $400 of the shared supplies ($1,000 x 40%) plus the $200 for the 100% business supplies, for a total supplies expense of $600.

Another way to track this on the *Redleaf Calendar-Keeper* is to create two expense categories for supplies. The supplies category already printed on the *Redleaf Calendar-Keeper* could be labeled "100% Supplies." The blank column next to it could be labeled "Shared Supplies." Supplies purchased throughout the year could be listed under the appropriate category. You should claim 100% of the supplies in the first category and the Time-Space percentage of the supplies in the second category. You can eliminate or combine the infrequently used expense categories shown on the calendar in order to have enough space to create the two expense categories that you need for your more frequent expenses.

How to Track Expenses When a Receipt Includes More Than One Expense Category

You can list all of the expenses from one receipt in one category, rather than splitting the receipt between two or more categories. For example, if a receipt has three toy items and two office-expense items, all of the expenses could be listed under either category. Simply decide which category to enter the total expense in and enter it once under that category. A more time-consuming option is to enter the date, check number, store name, and purchase amount for the office expenses on the first monthly expense report page, and the same information again, along with the purchase amount for the toys, on the second monthly expense report page. Either option will work, but remember, it is all added together in the end!

Child and Adult Care Food Program

Money received from the Food Program for children other than your own should be reported as income on your tax form. Money you receive for your own children, if you are income-eligible, is not taxable. Income from the Food Program can be recorded on either the attendance and payment log or the payment and income record. On the attendance and payment log, you can keep a monthly and year-to-date total of Food Program income, parent fees, and other income and still arrive at a year-to-date total income amount. This can help you track your income by category each year.

	FOOD PROGRAM INCOME RECVD	PARENT FEE INCOME RECVD	OTHER INCOME RECVD
FEBRUARY INCOME	$720	$1,500	—
BALANCE FORWARD	$710	$1,400	—
TOTAL Y-T-D INCOME	$1,430	$2,900	—

Using the *Redleaf Calendar-Keeper* with the Standard Meal Allowance Rule

You have two choices for claiming your food expenses. You can keep track of all business and personal food expenses and enter these amounts in the food column on the monthly expense report. Or you can use the standard meal allowance rule, which does not require you to track any food expenses or save any food receipts. For details about claiming food expenses, see the *Family Child Care Record-Keeping Guide*, 9th edition.

To use the standard meal allowance rule, you must maintain records that include the name of each child; the dates and hours of their attendance in care; and the number of breakfasts, lunches, dinners, and snacks served. How you can best use the *Redleaf Calendar-Keeper* to keep these records depends on whether you participate in the Food Program.

IF YOU ARE ON THE FOOD PROGRAM

Your monthly claim form contains all the information you need to track the reimbursed meals you served. Serving sizes for recipes in the *Redleaf Calendar-Keeper* are for ages three to five; adjust your serving according to the children in your care. Save these forms and put the totals on the year-end meal tally on page 95. You can also record the nonreimbursed meals and snacks you served on your monthly claim forms, or you can use the *Redleaf Calendar-Keeper* in one of two ways:

- Track nonreimbursed meals using the meal form on page 94. Photocopy this page, and use one form for each week of the year. You can also download this form at www.redleafpress.org (on the *Redleaf Calendar-Keeper* product page).
- Track nonreimbursed meals using the monthly attendance and payment log. On a separate line for each child, enter the number of nonreimbursed meals served, and total them at the bottom of the form each month.

IF YOU ARE NOT ON THE FOOD PROGRAM

Make sure you fill out the attendance and payment log each month with each child's name and his or her days and hours of attendance.

To track your meals and snacks, use the *Redleaf Calendar-Keeper* in one of two ways:

- Track all your meals and snacks using the meal form on page 94. Photocopy this page, and use one form for each week of the year. You can also download this form at www.redleafpress.org (on the *Redleaf Calendar-Keeper* product page).
- Track all your meals and snacks using the monthly attendance and payment log. On a separate line for each child, enter the number of meals and snacks served, and total them at the bottom of the form each month.

However you track your food expenses, enter the number of reimbursed and nonreimbursed meals on the year-end meal tally on page 95. Fill in the rest of the chart to calculate your food deduction.

How to Use the *Redleaf Calendar-Keeper* to Track Your Hours

There is a place at the top of each month's calendar to record and total the number of hours you care for children and the number of hours you work each month on business-related activities (such as cleaning, planning lessons, preparing meals, keeping records, and so on) when children are not present. A space to fill in your year-to-date total is also provided.

Carefully keeping track of the hours you work in your home will make the biggest difference in reducing your taxes. This is because your work hours are used in a Time-Space calculation that will determine how much of your house expenses you can deduct. These house expenses include your property tax, mortgage interest, utilities, homeowners insurance, house depreciation, house repairs, home improvements, and personal-property depreciation.

HOURS CHILDREN ARE IN YOUR HOME

Record all of the hours children are in your home on the attendance and payment log. You can also track irregular hours in the daily calendar squares. For example:

Carmen's normal hours are 7 AM to 5 PM. Total extra hours this week: 16 hours, 45 minutes

SUN	MON	TUE	WED	THU	FRI	SAT
	Sophia leaves 5:30 PM, 30 min.		James arrives 6:45 AM, 15 min.		Demi stays overnight, arrives 5 PM	Parents pick up Demi 9 AM, 16 hrs.

CLEANING, COOKING, AND PREPARING ACTIVITIES

The hours you spend preparing for your business when children are not present can be counted in the calculation of the Time-Space percentage. You may record these business hours in one of two ways. The first method is to mark your *Redleaf Calendar-Keeper* each time you are engaged in business activities. The IRS may challenge you by arguing that some of the hours reported were spent in personal activities. To avoid this, record personal activities separately. For example:

SUN	MON	TUE	WED	THU	FRI	SAT
4 PM, business cleaning, 1 hr. 5 PM, personal cleaning, 1 hr. 8 PM, business cooking, 1 hr.	7 PM, business cleaning, 1 hr.		7 AM, business cleaning, 1 hr. 7 PM, personal cleaning, 1 hr.	7 PM, business cooking, 30 min.	7 PM, business cleaning, 1 hr.	8:30 AM, plan trip to park, 30 min.

The second method is to prepare in advance a weekly or monthly schedule that indicates when you plan to spend time on business activities. Such a schedule is likely to be accepted by the IRS if it is kept regularly and followed carefully. You may use the *Redleaf Calendar-Keeper* to prepare your schedule, or you may write it out in a separate notebook. For example:

SUN	MON	TUE	WED	THU	FRI	SAT
1 PM, business cleaning, 1 hr. 2 PM, personal cleaning, 1 hr.	6 AM, business cleaning, 1 hr. 7 PM, personal cleaning, 1 hr.		7 PM, personal cleaning, 1 hr. 8 PM, business cooking, 1 hr.		7 PM, personal cleaning, 1 hr.	

Note: You can detail your plans for one week in the month and let it represent what you will do every week in the month.

PARENT INTERVIEWS AND PHONE CALLS

Record the amount of time you spend outside of regular business hours interviewing parents or talking to parents on the phone.

RECORD KEEPING

Record the time you spend record keeping, planning menus, preparing shopping lists, balancing your checkbook, or doing financial bookkeeping for your business. For example:

SUN	MON	TUE	WED	THU	FRI	SAT
1 8 AM, balance checkbook, 30 min.	2	3 7 AM, talk to Hugo's mother, 15 min.	4	5	6 5 PM, interview the Bzdoks, 1 hr.	7 9 PM, plan menus, 1 hr.
8 10 PM, call from Sia's father, Sia is ill, 20 min.	9	10	11	12	13	14 9 PM, plan menus, 1 hr.

Notes on Record Keeping
- Review the record-keeping notes on your *Redleaf Calendar-Keeper* at the end of each month to make sure you recorded all your business activities.
- You may not count hours spent away from your home in your Time-Space percentage. This includes time spent shopping or transporting children to school.
- Do not count hours spent on business activities while children are in your care.

For a complete explanation of the Time-Space percentage, refer to chapter 3 of the *Family Child Care Record-Keeping Guide*, 9th edition. (For information about the *Family Child Care Record-Keeping Guide*, 9th edition, see page 66 of the *Redleaf Calendar-Keeper*.)

Attendance and Payment Log

Here are some examples of ways to use the attendance and payment log. Remember, the system to use is the one that works best for you.

EXAMPLE A

Provider has steady attendance, both full-time and part-time child care, but no drop-ins. She is paid whether the child is there or not.

Method 1: Provider enters drop-off and pickup times and records total hours in attendance. Payments are recorded on the payment and income record or on the attendance and payment log. This is the preferred method if you are using the IRS standard meal allowance rate because it shows when children are present.

Method 2: Provider checks (✓) attendance and records total hours in attendance. Parent payments are recorded in the same way as Method 1.

Method 3: Provider writes in total hours in attendance every day and records weekly payment in the TOTAL column of the attendance and payment log.

EXAMPLE B

Provider does only part-time child care. She is paid by the hour.

Method 1: Provider enters drop-off and pickup times and records total hours in attendance. Payments are recorded on the payment and income record or on the attendance and payment log.

Method 2: Provider uses two lines, noting drop-off and pickup times on the first line, totaling the number of hours in attendance each day on the second line and recording the total hours in attendance each week in the Saturday column. Payments are recorded in the TOTAL column of the attendance and payment log or on the payment and income record.

JANUARY ATTENDANCE AND PAYMENT LOG

CHILD'S NAME	S	M	T	W	T	F	S	TOTAL
Prudence		7/5	7/5	7/5	7/5	7/5		50hrs / $300

CHILD'S NAME	S	M	T	W	T	F	S	TOTAL
Prudence		✓	✓	✓	✓	✓		50hrs / $300

CHILD'S NAME	S	M	T	W	T	F	S	TOTAL
Prudence		10	10	10	10	10		50hrs / $300

CHILD'S NAME	S	M	T	W	T	F	S	TOTAL HRS
Carmen			3/5		3/6			5
TJ		8/10		8/10				4

	S	M	T	W	T	F	S	
Carmen			3/5		3/6			
			2	3			5	$30
TJ		8/10		8/10				
		2		2			4	$24

PAYMENT AND INCOME RECORD FOR JANUARY

CHILD'S NAME	JANUARY					JAN TOTAL
	2	8	15	22	29	
Carmen	$30					
TJ	$24					

EXAMPLE C

Provider has a steady full-time child (Prudence), a steady part-time child (TJ), and a drop-in child (Hasan). She uses a combination of methods—Example A, Method 3 (Prudence) and Example B, Method 1 (TJ and Hasan).

CHILD'S NAME	S	M	T	W	T	F	S	TOTAL HRS
Prudence		10	10	10	10	10		50
TJ		8/10		8/10		8/10		6
Hasan			1/4					3

House Expenses Worksheet—see page 84

This chart is designed for recording your utilities and other home expenses. Space is provided for you to record the portion of these expenses that can be claimed as business expenses on your federal income tax return.

Income Tax Worksheet—see page 85

After totaling your expenses for December, enter the yearly amounts on the income tax worksheet. From here you can easily transfer your expenses to the Schedule C.

Payment and Income Record—see pages 86–93

These eight pages for recording your income are an alternative to the attendance and payment log. You can use the attendance and payment log to record attendance only and use the payment and income record to record income. To use these pages, write in the date you expect parents to pay you. In the correct space, record the amount (and the check number) and then the total for the month. At the bottom of the page, include Food Program income and any other income you receive. For the second, third, and fourth quarters, a space is provided for the balance carried forward. A paper clip or piece of tape on the edge of the current payment and income record page will make it easy to find in the *Redleaf Calendar-Keeper*.

PAYMENT AND INCOME RECORD FOR JANUARY

CHILD'S NAME	JANUARY					JAN TOTAL
	2	8	15	22	29	
Carmen	4130 $62.00	4229 59.00	4275 89.00	4301 75.00	4362 68.00	353.00
TJ	Cash 50.00	Cash 50.00	Cash 50.00	Cash 50.00	Cash 50.00	250.00

Emergency Phone Numbers—see pages 96 and 97

Although you should have additional information for each child, this form provides quick access to the basic information. You may want to make a photocopy of this sheet to take with you on outings or field trips. There are lines for your own address and phone number because this information may be needed in an emergency, and you may not be the person making the emergency phone call.

Emergency Drill Record—see page 98

The emergency drill record will help you stay organized and keep an accurate record of this important routine. There is space to record a fire drill and one other emergency drill (for example, storm, tornado, or earthquake) for each month. Faithful practice and good records help keep everyone safe.

Published by Redleaf Press
10 Yorkton Court
St. Paul, MN 55117
www.redleafpress.org

© 2026 by Redleaf Press

All rights reserved. Unless otherwise noted on a specific page, no portion of this publication may be reproduced or transmitted in any form or by any means, electronic or mechanical, including photocopying, recording, or capturing on any information storage and retrieval system, without permission in writing from the publisher, except by a reviewer, who may quote brief passages in a critical article or review to be printed in a magazine or newspaper, or electronically transmitted on radio, television, or the internet.

Forty-ninth edition 2026
Senior editor: Melissa York
Cover design: Renee Hammes
Cover image © Adobe Stock
Printed in the United States of America
ISBN 978-1-60554-868-5

Redleaf Press is the publishing division of Think Small.

Please note: Because dates for certain holidays change from year to year, we cannot guarantee their accuracy. Check with your local library if you have questions. The observance of all Jewish and Islamic holidays begins at sundown the previous day.

Redleaf Press®
www.redleafpress.org
800-423-8309

JANUARY 2026

	Hours Worked
Previous Total	
No. Hours Open*	
Other Hours Worked**	
Year-to-Date Total	

* "No. Hours Open" refers to hours from when the first child arrived to when the last child left (not your advertised work hours).
** "Other Hours Worked" refers to hours spent on business activities in the home (cleaning, meal preparation, activity planning, and so on) when children are not present.

SUN	MON	TUE	WED	THU	FRI	SAT
DECEMBER 2025	FEBRUARY 2026		Are you ready for tax season? Order your 2025 tax products now!	**1** New Year's Day	**2**	**3**
4	**5** Fire Drill Day — Record your vehicle's odometer reading	**6**	**7**	**8**	**9**	**10**
11	**12**	**13**	**14** Severe Storm Drill Day	**15** 2025 4th quarter estimated taxes due	**16**	**17**
18	**19** Martin Luther King Jr. Day	**20**	**21**	**22**	**23**	**24**
25	**26**	**27**	**28**	**29**	**30** Call your local R & R agency; update your service	**31**

JANUARY

Navigating Transitions

Greetings, snack, then time to play—
Routines take us through our day!

Recipes

Orange Cranberry Quick Bread

1⅓ cups fresh or frozen unsweetened cranberries
⅓ cup sugar, divided
1 cup whole wheat flour
¼ teaspoon baking powder
¼ teaspoon baking soda
⅛ teaspoon salt
1 egg
⅓ cup unsweetened applesauce
1 teaspoon orange extract

1. Preheat oven to 350° F. Spray an 8½ x 4½–inch loaf pan with nonstick cooking spray.
2. In a small bowl, combine cranberries and 2 tablespoons of sugar. Toss and set aside.
3. In a medium bowl, combine flour, remaining sugar, baking powder, baking soda, and salt. Whisk to mix well.
4. In a separate small bowl, combine egg, applesauce, and orange extract. Whisk until well blended. Add wet ingredients to the dry ingredients and mix. Fold the cranberries into the dough.
5. Pour dough into loaf pan and bake for 50–55 minutes.

Yield: 6 servings
Meal Component: Grain

Collard Greens

2 tablespoons (about 1 slice) turkey bacon, chopped
½ cup diced onions
2 quarts chopped collard greens
¼ teaspoon liquid smoke (optional)

1. Coat a medium stockpot with nonstick cooking spray and heat over medium heat. Heat bacon for 3–4 minutes, until lightly brown, stirring frequently.

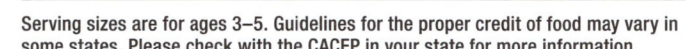
Serving sizes are for ages 3–5. Guidelines for the proper credit of food may vary in some states. Please check with the CACFP in your state for more information.

Menu of the Month

Breakfast
Milk
Orange Cranberry Quick Bread* (WG)
Canned Peaches

Morning Snack
Water
Hummus
Whole Grain Pitas (WG)

Lunch
Milk
Collard Greens*
Grilled Chicken Breasts
Whole Grain Roll (WG)
Oranges

Afternoon Snack
Apple Slices
Cheese Cubes

*Indicates recipes of the month.
(WG) Indicates whole grain.
Recipes adapted from the Institute of Childhood Nutrition.

2. Increase heat to medium-high. Add onions and sauté until soft. Add collard greens. Sauté for 1–2 minutes, stirring continuously, until greens begin to wilt.
3. Add 1 cup water to stockpot, cover, and bring to a boil. Reduce heat to medium. Simmer for 5–7 minutes, stirring occasionally. Stir in liquid smoke (optional). Remove from heat when greens are tender.

Yield: 6 servings, ⅓ cup each
Meal Component: Vegetable

Nutrition and Fitness Notes

Establish a routine when preparing for rest time. Encourage children to help with placing cots and getting their sheets or blankets from their individual storage spaces. Lowering the lights and playing soft music can create a soothing environment. Read, sing quietly, or provide other relaxation activities leading into and during rest time.

The Experienced Provider

Be mindful of transitions in your curriculum planning. Throughout the day, the children will transition many times. Some of the transitions include drop off, restroom breaks, handwashing, choosing learning areas, cleaning up, outdoor play, mealtimes, and pick-up. Plan ahead of time for each transition from one activity or location to the next. Give the children something to do, such as counting or singing. Only implement transitions appropriate for the developmental levels of the children currently participating in the program.

Activities for Children

Wave Bye-Bye
Infants often have a hard time making transitions from a family member to a caregiver. Transitions from one place to another can also be hard. You can support them in their transitions by encouraging them to wave and/or say "bye-bye" to the person, place, or objects they are leaving. For example, when it is time to come inside after a fun time in the play yard, say "bye-bye" to the swing and sand and invite the infants to wave bye-bye.

Planning with Children
Including children as you develop your weekly plan or your daily schedule of activities helps build their sense of agency and belief in themselves. Try asking children what they would like to learn. You may be surprised at the response. Encourage children to change the rules of a game or allow them to change the objective of an activity when appropriate. Let children know you respect their opinions, and challenge them to come up with new ideas for old games.

Visual Supports
Use visual supports such as visual schedules, picture cards, and labels to help children understand routines and expectations. Use individualized strategies by adjusting routines. Provide flexible schedules and transitions tailored to individual needs.

Literacy Corner

All in One Day by Mike Huber
Follow along as an ordinary day in Mr. Walter's classroom turns into something unexpected. This story showcases the routine of the day in one group-care setting.

Bye-Bye Time by Elizabeth Verdick
This gentle book helps ease the transition and avoid separation anxiety with simple rituals: hugs and kisses, a big wave, a deep breath, and the confidence to seek comfort with the new caregiver or other children.

JANUARY ATTENDANCE AND PAYMENT LOG

To record drop-off and pickup times that vary, try using two lines per child.

CHILD'S NAME	S	M	T	W	T 1	F 2	S 3	TOTAL	S 4	M 5	T 6	W 7	T 8	F 9	S 10	TOTAL	S 11	M 12	T 13	W 14	T 15	F 16	S 17	TOTAL	S 18	M 19	T 20	W 21	T 22	F 23	S 24	TOTAL	S 25	M 26	T 27	W 28	T 29	F 30	S 31	TOTAL	S	M

JANUARY ATTENDANCE AND PAYMENT LOG CONTINUED

CHILD'S NAME	S	M	T 1	W 2	T 3	F	S	TOTAL	S 4	M 5	T 6	W 7	T 8	F 9	S 10	TOTAL	S 11	M 12	T 13	W 14	T 15	F 16	S 17	TOTAL	S 18	M 19	T 20	W 21	T 22	F 23	S 24	TOTAL	S 25	M 26	T 27	W 28	T 29	F 30	S 31	TOTAL	S	M

WEEKLY PAYMENT TOTALS

	FOOD PROGRAM INCOME RECVD	PARENT FEE INCOME RECVD	OTHER INCOME RECVD			
JANUARY INCOME*				=	JAN TOTAL	
BALANCE FORWARD				=	BALANCE FWD TOTAL	
TOTAL Y-T-D INCOME				=	TOTAL Y-T-D	

Food Program Claim

Date Claim Sent _____

Date Check Received _____

MEAL COUNT TALLY

BREAKFASTS	
LUNCHES	
DINNERS	
SNACKS	

*Include income received in January 2025 for meals served in 2024.

Put totals in year-end meal tally, page 95.

JANUARY EXPENSE REPORT

DATE	PAYMENT TYPE cash, check #, cc #, debit	PURCHASED FROM	PURCHASE TOTAL	ADVERTISING	INSURANCE	INTEREST	LEGAL & PROFESSIONAL SERVICES	OFFICE EXPENSES (including internet & 2nd phone)	RENT OF BUSINESS PROPERTY	REPAIR & MAINTENANCE	SUPPLIES		MILES
		THIS MONTH'S TOTAL											
		BALANCE CARRIED FORWARD											
		YEAR-TO-DATE TOTAL											

JANUARY EXPENSE REPORT

DATE	PAYMENT TYPE cash, check #, cc #, debit	PURCHASED FROM	PURCHASE TOTAL	TAXES & LICENSES	TRAVEL & ENTERTAINMENT	FOOD	TOYS	HOUSEHOLD ITEMS	CLEANING SUPPLIES	ACTIVITY EXPENSES			MILES
			THIS MONTH'S TOTAL										
			BALANCE CARRIED FORWARD										
			YEAR-TO-DATE TOTAL										

See page 85 for an explanation of how to transfer expenses to your tax forms. You may wish to relabel the columns to fit your business needs.

See page 6 for an explanation of the order in which we present the categories.

FEBRUARY 2026

* "No. Hours Open" refers to hours from when the first child arrived to when the last child left (not your advertised work hours).
** "Other Hours Worked" refers to hours spent on business activities in the home (cleaning, meal preparation, activity planning, and so on) when children are not present.

Hours Worked
Previous Total
No. Hours Open*
Other Hours Worked**
Year-to-Date Total

SUN	MON	TUE	WED	THU	FRI	SAT
1 Black History Month Dental Health Month	**2** Groundhog Day Fire Drill Day	**3**	**4**	**5**	**6**	**7**
8	**9**	**10**	**11** Severe Storm Drill Day	**12**	**13**	**14** Valentine's Day
15	**16** Presidents' Day	**17** Mardi Gras Chinese New Year	**18** Ash Wednesday (Christian) Ramadan begins (Islamic)	**19**	**20**	**21**
22	**23**	**24**	**25**	**26**	**27** Call your local R & R agency; update your service	**28**

JANUARY 2026

S	M	T	W	T	F	S
				1	2	3
4	5	6	7	8	9	10
11	12	13	14	15	16	17
18	19	20	21	22	23	24
25	26	27	28	29	30	31

MARCH 2026

S	M	T	W	T	F	S
1	2	3	4	5	6	7
8	9	10	11	12	13	14
15	16	17	18	19	20	21
22	23	24	25	26	27	28
29	30	31				

FEBRUARY

We Love Our Families

With letters, art, and stories we share,
We show our families that we care.

Recipes

Chicken and Egg Noodle Soup

2 teaspoons canola oil
1 cup diced onions
½ teaspoon ground ginger
1 clove garlic, minced
9¼ ounces cooked and diced chicken breast
5 cups low-sodium chicken broth
2 tablespoons low-sodium soy sauce
3 ounces uncooked stir-fry/Chinese egg noodles
1½ cups shredded fresh cabbage
1 quart fresh baby spinach
¼ cup chopped green onions
½ teaspoon sesame oil

1. Heat canola oil in a medium pot over medium-high heat. Add onions and cook for 3 minutes or until onions are soft. Stir in ginger, garlic, and salt and pepper to taste. Cook for 1 minute or until ginger and garlic become fragrant.
2. Add chicken, chicken broth, and soy sauce. Bring to a boil, and continue cooking for 5–7 minutes. Stir in noodles and cabbage. Cook for 4 minutes or until noodles are soft.
3. Stir in spinach, green onions, and sesame oil. Remove from heat.

Yield: 6 servings, 1¼ cups each
Meal Component: Meat/Meat Alternate, Vegetable, Grain

Fruit and Nut Butter Pita Pockets

3 whole wheat pita rounds, at least 1 oz each
6 tablespoons smooth peanut butter
1 medium apple, cut into 12 slices
1 large pear, cut into 12 slices

Serving sizes are for ages 3–5. Guidelines for the proper credit of food may vary in some states. Please check with the CACFP in your state for more information.

Menu of the Month

Breakfast
Milk
Scrambled Eggs
Red Pepper Slices

Morning Snack
100% Orange Juice
Whole Wheat Toast (WG)

Lunch
Milk
Chicken and Egg Noodle Soup*
Kiwi Slices

Afternoon Snack
Water
Fruit and Nut Butter Pita Pockets* (WG)

*Indicates recipes of the month.
(WG) Indicates whole grain.
Recipes adapted from the Institute of Childhood Nutrition.

1. Cut each pita round in half. Spread 1 tablespoon of peanut butter in each pita pocket half.
2. Place 2 pieces of apple and 2 pieces of pear in each pita pocket half.

Yield: 6 servings, ½ pita each
Meal Component: Meat/Meat Alternate, Grain

Nutrition and Fitness Notes

Become familiar with the families of children in your care and in the community. Food choices, preparation methods, and eating habits are often influenced by culture and religious beliefs. Encourage and model respect for food choices.

The Experienced Provider

Parental involvement decreases as children get older. Adults in general may assume children's increasing independence means they require less attention and adult-child interaction. Encouraging the parents and caregivers of the children enrolled in your program to engage in educational activities with their children at all ages can combat many of the negative influential factors on child development.

Activities for Children

Love and Snuggles
The more a child is cuddled, snuggled, and held, the more secure and independent that child will become. Young children, especially infants, need to be held often for bonding and normal brain development to occur. Be sure to allow sufficient time in the day to snuggle and hold infants. While holding an infant in your arms, walk or rock the child back and forth while talking softly to him. With older children, snuggle while reading a book, hold hands while going for a walk, and give hugs when they are needed.

Family Music
Ask families the names of songs they listen to in their homes. After compiling the responses, make a playlist with some of the songs. During large-group time, the class can dance to the different music. Children will be pleasantly surprised to hear music from their homes played at school.

Family Languages
Encouraging and supporting bilingualism and multilingual families promotes community and belonging in your family child care program. Engaging children in conversations in their home language or consistently immersing commonly used languages into each day supports brain development. While it's not necessary to learn to fluently speak the languages of each of the families and children in your program, families will appreciate you learning and expressing general greetings, salutations, and frequently used action words in the language they speak.

Literacy Corner

A Family Is a Family Is a Family by Sara O'Leary
When a teacher asks the children in her class to think about what makes their families special, the answers are all different in many ways—but the same in the one way that matters most of all.

Who's in My Family? All About Families by Robie H. Harris
Join Nellie and Gus and their family—plus all manner of other families—for a day at the zoo, where they see animal families galore!

FEBRUARY ATTENDANCE AND PAYMENT LOG

To record drop-off and pickup times that vary, try using two lines per child.

CHILD'S NAME	S 1	M 2	T 3	W 4	T 5	F 6	S 7	TOTAL	S 8	M 9	T 10	W 11	T 12	F 13	S 14	TOTAL	S 15	M 16	T 17	W 18	T 19	F 20	S 21	TOTAL	S 22	M 23	T 24	W 25	T 26	F 27	S 28	TOTAL	S	M	T	W	T	F	S	TOTAL	S	M	

FEBRUARY ATTENDANCE AND PAYMENT LOG CONTINUED

CHILD'S NAME	S 1	M 2	T 3	W 4	T 5	F 6	S 7	TOTAL	S 8	M 9	T 10	W 11	T 12	F 13	S 14	TOTAL	S 15	M 16	T 17	W 18	T 19	F 20	S 21	TOTAL	S 22	M 23	T 24	W 25	T 26	F 27	S 28	TOTAL	S	M	T	W	T	F	S	TOTAL	S	M

WEEKLY PAYMENT TOTALS

	FOOD PROGRAM INCOME RECVD	PARENT FEE INCOME RECVD	OTHER INCOME RECVD			
FEBRUARY INCOME				=	FEB TOTAL	
BALANCE FORWARD				=	BALANCE FWD TOTAL	
TOTAL Y-T-D INCOME				=	TOTAL Y-T-D	

Food Program Claim

Date Claim Sent _____

Date Check Received _____

MEAL COUNT TALLY	
BREAKFASTS	
LUNCHES	
DINNERS	
SNACKS	

Put totals in year-end meal tally, page 95.

FEBRUARY EXPENSE REPORT

DATE	PAYMENT TYPE cash, check #, cc #, debit	PURCHASED FROM	PURCHASE TOTAL	ADVERTISING	INSURANCE	INTEREST	LEGAL & PROFESSIONAL SERVICES	OFFICE EXPENSES (including internet & 2nd phone)	RENT OF BUSINESS PROPERTY	REPAIR & MAINTENANCE	SUPPLIES		MILES
		THIS MONTH'S TOTAL											
		BALANCE CARRIED FORWARD											
		YEAR-TO-DATE TOTAL											

FEBRUARY EXPENSE REPORT

DATE	PAYMENT TYPE cash, check #, cc #, debit	PURCHASED FROM	PURCHASE TOTAL	TAXES & LICENSES	TRAVEL & ENTERTAINMENT	FOOD	TOYS	HOUSEHOLD ITEMS	CLEANING SUPPLIES	ACTIVITY EXPENSES			MILES
		THIS MONTH'S TOTAL											
		BALANCE CARRIED FORWARD											
		YEAR-TO-DATE TOTAL											

See page 85 for an explanation of how to transfer expenses to your tax forms. You may wish to relabel the columns to fit your business needs.

See page 6 for an explanation of the order in which we present the categories.

MARCH 2026

	Hours Worked
	Previous Total
	No. Hours Open*
	Other Hours Worked**
	Year-to-Date Total

* "No. Hours Open" refers to hours from when the first child arrived to when the last child left (not your advertised work hours).
** "Other Hours Worked" refers to hours spent on business activities in the home (cleaning, meal preparation, activity planning, and so on) when children are not present.

SUN	MON	TUE	WED	THU	FRI	SAT
1 National Women's History Month; National Nutrition Month; National Reading Month	**2** Read Across America Day; Fire Drill Day	**3** Purim (Jewish)	**4**	**5**	**6**	**7**
8	**9**	**10**	**11** Severe Storm Drill Day	**12**	**13**	**14**
15	**16**	**17** St. Patrick's Day	**18**	**19** Ramadan ends (Islamic)	**20** Eid al-Fitr (Islamic); Spring begins; Change your smoke alarms and carbon monoxide filter batteries	**21**
22	**23**	**24**	**25**	**26**	**27**	**28**
29 Palm Sunday (Christian)	**30**	**31** Call your local R & R agency; update your service				

FEBRUARY 2026

S	M	T	W	T	F	S
1	2	3	4	5	6	7
8	9	10	11	12	13	14
15	16	17	18	19	20	21
22	23	24	25	26	27	28

APRIL 2026

S	M	T	W	T	F	S
			1	2	3	4
5	6	7	8	9	10	11
12	13	14	15	16	17	18
19	20	21	22	23	24	25
26	27	28	29	30		

MARCH

Everyday Science

Science fun is all around—
In kitchen, backyard, and playground!

Recipes

Strawberry and Waffle Kebobs

¾ cup nonfat vanilla Greek yogurt
1 tablespoon maple syrup
3 frozen whole grain-rich waffles, at least 1 ounce each
3 cups whole strawberries (about 36)

1. Gather 12 sticks for kebabs. In a small bowl, whisk yogurt and maple syrup until well blended.
2. Lightly toast waffles for 3–4 minutes. Cut each waffle into 4 triangles.
3. Build 12 kebabs with 3 strawberries and 1 waffle triangle each. Serve 2 kebabs with 2 tablespoons of maple-yogurt dip.

Yield: 6 servings, 2 kebabs each
Meal Component: Fruit, Grain

Honey Lime Chicken

1 pound, 7 ounces raw boneless, skinless chicken thighs
⅓ cup honey
¼ cup fresh lime juice
⅛ cup lime zest

1. Combine chicken thighs, honey, lime juice, lime zest, and salt and pepper to taste in a large bowl. Stir well. Allow flavors to blend for 15–20 minutes in the refrigerator.
2. Preheat oven to 400° F. Place seasoned chicken thighs on a baking pan lightly coated with pan release spray and lined with parchment paper. Bake for 30–35 minutes. Heat to an internal temperature of 165° F. Once chicken thighs are removed from oven, cut into one-quarter inch cubes.

Yield: 6 servings, ⅓ cup each
Meal Component: Meat/Meat Alternate

Serving sizes are for ages 3–5. Guidelines for the proper credit of food may vary in some states. Please check with the CACFP in your state for more information.

Menu of the Month

Breakfast
Milk
Strawberry and Waffle Kebobs* (WG)

Morning Snack
Water
Whole Wheat Raisin Bread (WG)
Cottage Cheese

Lunch
Milk
Honey Lime Chicken*
Brown Rice (WG)
Steamed Mixed Frozen Vegetables
Applesauce

Afternoon Snack
Cantaloupe Chunks
Whole Grain Pretzels (WG)

*Indicates recipes of the month.
(WG) Indicates whole grain.
Recipes adapted from the Institute of Childhood Nutrition.

Nutrition and Fitness Notes

Help the children select and cut pictures from magazines of the following food groups: bread and grains; milk and milk products; fruit; vegetables; meat, beans, and nuts. Tell the children to choose something from each category to paste onto a paper plate. Tell them that to be healthy, they must eat some of each of these kinds of foods every day.

The Experienced Provider

Loose parts create science-rich environments for children to engage, notice, wonder, and question. Scientific inquiry expands as children transform, transfer, and transport materials in an open-ended way. Like scientists, children develop hypotheses, try them out, and experiment with materials through trial and error. The science inquiry skills children acquire through loose parts play equip them to attain deeper understanding of science concepts.

Activities for Children

The Science of Blocks
Blocks provide many developmental opportunities in early child care. Encourage older children to build towers with blocks to demonstrate to toddlers how this is done. Watch closely so toddlers do not become frustrated or bored. If they are unable to stack the blocks, allow them to find another activity and try again later. While toddlers are building their towers, talk about the concepts of top and bottom. Place a small toy on the top of the block tower and explain how it is on top. Knock the toy off and explain to the toddlers that it is now on the bottom. Repeat the game, allowing the children to move the toy from top to bottom.

Nature Scientists
Take a walk around the block or to a nearby park with the children and ask them to share the smells, sounds, and things they see. Record their observations and display the paper where the children can see it. A few days or a week later, take the same walk and ask the children to make observations again. Compare the new notes with the ones from the first walk. Ask the children what was the same, what was different, and why they think it was different. Before taking the walk a third time, ask the children to reflect on the first two walks and make predictions about their observations.

Be Melanin
For this activity, prepare cards with different skin colors on them and a music playlist with songs of various tempos. In the book *All the Colors We Are: The Story of How We Get Our Skin Color*, author Katie Kissinger explains variations in skin hues by how active someone's melanin is. Tell children that they will move their bodies more quickly for colors that have more active melanin and more slowly for colors that have less active melanin. Hold up a color with more active melanin and play an up-tempo song. Then hold up a skin color with less active melanin and play a slow song. Play songs that are neither fast nor slow for mid skin tones.

Literacy Corner

No Two Alike by Keith Baker
Follow a pair of birds on a snowflake-filled journey through a gorgeous winter landscape to explore how everything everywhere is wonderfully unique—from branches and leaves to forests and trees to friends and loved ones.

All the Colors We Are: The Story of How We Get Our Skin Color by Katie Kissinger
Celebrate the essence of one way we are all special and different from one another—our skin color! Colorful photographs and engaging text help children understand why our skin comes in a rainbow of colors.

MARCH ATTENDANCE AND PAYMENT LOG

To record drop-off and pickup times that vary, try using two lines per child.

CHILD'S NAME	S 1	M 2	T 3	W 4	T 5	F 6	S 7	TOTAL	S 8	M 9	T 10	W 11	T 12	F 13	S 14	TOTAL	S 15	M 16	T 17	W 18	T 19	F 20	S 21	TOTAL	S 22	M 23	T 24	W 25	T 26	F 27	S 28	TOTAL	S 29	M 30	T 31	W	T	F	S	TOTAL	S	M

MARCH ATTENDANCE AND PAYMENT LOG CONTINUED

CHILD'S NAME	S 1	M 2	T 3	W 4	T 5	F 6	S 7	TOTAL	S 8	M 9	T 10	W 11	T 12	F 13	S 14	TOTAL	S 15	M 16	T 17	W 18	T 19	F 20	S 21	TOTAL	S 22	M 23	T 24	W 25	T 26	F 27	S 28	TOTAL	S 29	M 30	T 31	W	T	F	S	TOTAL	S	M

WEEKLY PAYMENT TOTALS

	FOOD PROGRAM INCOME RECVD	PARENT FEE INCOME RECVD	OTHER INCOME RECVD			
MARCH INCOME				=	MAR TOTAL	
BALANCE FORWARD				=	BALANCE FWD TOTAL	
TOTAL Y-T-D INCOME				=	TOTAL Y-T-D	

Food Program Claim

Date Claim Sent _____

Date Check Received _____

MEAL COUNT TALLY

BREAKFASTS	
LUNCHES	
DINNERS	
SNACKS	

Put totals in year-end meal tally, page 95.

MARCH EXPENSE REPORT

DATE	PAYMENT TYPE cash, check #, cc #, debit	PURCHASED FROM	PURCHASE TOTAL	ADVERTISING	INSURANCE	INTEREST	LEGAL & PROFESSIONAL SERVICES	OFFICE EXPENSES (including internet & 2nd phone)	RENT OF BUSINESS PROPERTY	REPAIR & MAINTENANCE	SUPPLIES		MILES
		THIS MONTH'S TOTAL											
		BALANCE CARRIED FORWARD											
		YEAR-TO-DATE TOTAL											

MARCH EXPENSE REPORT

DATE	PAYMENT TYPE cash, check #, cc #, debit	PURCHASED FROM	PURCHASE TOTAL	TAXES & LICENSES	TRAVEL & ENTERTAINMENT	FOOD	TOYS	HOUSEHOLD ITEMS	CLEANING SUPPLIES	ACTIVITY EXPENSES			MILES
		THIS MONTH'S TOTAL											
		BALANCE CARRIED FORWARD											
		YEAR-TO-DATE TOTAL											

See page 85 for an explanation of how to transfer expenses to your tax forms.
You may wish to relabel the columns to fit your business needs.

See page 6 for an explanation of the order in which we present the categories.

APRIL 2026

* "No. Hours Open" refers to hours from when the first child arrived to when the last child left (not your advertised work hours).
** "Other Hours Worked" refers to hours spent on business activities in the home (cleaning, meal preparation, activity planning, and so on) when children are not present.

Hours Worked
Previous Total
No. Hours Open*
Other Hours Worked**
Year-to-Date Total

SUN	MON	TUE	WED	THU	FRI	SAT
MARCH 2026 / MAY 2026			**1** April Fools' Day / National Child Abuse Prevention Month	**2** Passover begins (Jewish)	**3** Good Friday (Christian)	**4**
5 Easter Sunday (Christian)	**6** Week of the Young Child / Fire Drill Day	**7**	**8** Severe Storm Drill Day	**9** Passover ends (Jewish)	**10** National Siblings Day	**11**
12 Orthodox Easter (Orthodox)	**13**	**14**	**15** 2025 income taxes due / 2026 1st quarter estimated taxes due	**16**	**17**	**18**
19 Patriots' Day	**20**	**21**	**22** Earth Day	**23**	**24** Arbor Day	**25**
26	**27**	**28**	**29**	**30** Call your local R & R agency; update your service		

APRIL

Moving and Growing
We crawl, walk, run, and hop along
Moving our bodies makes us strong!

Recipes

Quiche with Self-Forming Crust
8 ounces frozen whole eggs, thawed
1½ cups nonfat milk
½ cup whole wheat flour
¼ teaspoon baking powder
2 cups diced onions
2 cups diced red bell peppers
2 cups chopped fresh spinach
⅓ cup shredded low-fat cheddar cheese

1. Preheat oven to 375°F. Pour eggs into a mixer and mix on low speed for 2 minutes. Add milk, flour, baking powder, and salt and pepper to taste. Mix for 4 minutes on low speed.
2. Combine onions, peppers, spinach, and egg mixture in a large mixing bowl. Stir well.
3. Pour egg and vegetable mixture into an 8-by-8-inch baking dish lightly coated with pan release spray. Sprinkle cheese over egg mixture. Bake for 35 minutes. Heat to an internal temperature of 165°F.

Yield: 6 packets
Meal Component: Meat/Meat Alternate, Vegetable

Cheesy Bean Tostada
¾ cup fat-free, low-sodium refried beans
6 corn tortillas, at least ½ ounce each
6 tablespoons reduced-fat, shredded cheddar cheese

1. Preheat oven to 400°F. Spread 2 tablespoons of beans on each corn tortilla. Sprinkle 1 tablespoon of cheese evenly over the beans on each tortilla.
2. Place on ungreased baking sheet and bake for 7 minutes or until cheese is melted.

Yield: 6 servings
Meal Component: Meat/Meat Alternate, Grain

Menu of the Month

Breakfast
Milk
Quiche with Self-Forming Crust*

Morning Snack
Cucumbers
Whole Grain Popcorn (WG)

Lunch
Milk
Turkey and Cheese Sandwiches
Canned Mandarin Oranges
Baby Carrots

Afternoon Snack
Water
Cheesy Bean Tostada* (WG)

*Indicates recipes of the month.
(WG) Indicates whole grain.
Recipes adapted from the Institute of Childhood Nutrition.

Nutrition and Fitness Notes

Physical activities that promote large-muscle development for all age groups are necessary parts of any family child care's daily schedule: running and jumping, throwing and catching, walking and skipping. Gross-motor skill development is necessary for infants as well as older children in your program. Exercises and games that provide for large-muscle development in infants will assist in their ability to roll over, crawl, and eventually take their first steps.

The Experienced Provider

Most children are eager to walk, run, climb, or move to the maximum of their ability. Introducing safety gates and creating fall-safe environments (carpeting, blankets, pillows, and so on) are ways to minimize injury. Create environments that acknowledge how young children develop while continuing to keep them safe. Restraining young children in a manner that impedes their development is not a legitimate safety plan.

Activities for Children

In Balance
Clear a wide area indoors or outdoors. Place a 4-foot length of string on the floor or use chalk to draw a line outside. Invite children to participate in balance-themed challenges. Model how to stand on one foot and exaggerate how you use your arms to help keep your balance. If the children are easily able to stand on one foot, ask them to try to hop on one foot. Next, invite the children to walk heel to toe on the string or chalk line. Ask an older child to show the children how to do this or model it yourself.

Learning to Push
Select several items for the infant to push. Choose lightweight objects such as a stuffed animal, a small toy, and a push toy. Start the activity by saying, "One, two, three," and then push one of the toys. Repeat the counting and encourage the infant to do the pushing. You may demonstrate how the push toy can be used as a carriage to transport the other toys.

Accessible Spaces
Create an inclusive environment by designing activities and spaces to be accessible for all children, with options for various learning styles and abilities. Adapt materials by modifying toys, books, or activities to ensure they are usable by children with differing abilities (adding textures, using larger items, and so forth).

Literacy Corner

From Head to Toe by Eric Carle
Giraffes can bend their necks, monkeys can wave their hands, and donkeys can kick their legs. And so can you! Throughout this interactive board book, the animals invite young readers to copy their antics as they play.

I Will Dance by Nancy Bo Flood
Eva longs to dance. But unlike many would-be dancers, Eva has cerebral palsy. She doesn't know what dance looks like for someone who uses a wheelchair. Then Eva learns of a place that has created a class for dancers of all abilities.

Serving sizes are for ages 3–5. Guidelines for the proper credit of food may vary in some states. Please check with the CACFP in your state for more information.

APRIL ATTENDANCE AND PAYMENT LOG

To record drop-off and pickup times that vary, try using two lines per child.

CHILD'S NAME	S	M	T	W 1	T 2	F 3	S 4	TOTAL	S 5	M 6	T 7	W 8	T 9	F 10	S 11	TOTAL	S 12	M 13	T 14	W 15	T 16	F 17	S 18	TOTAL	S 19	M 20	T 21	W 22	T 23	F 24	S 25	TOTAL	S 26	M 27	T 28	W 29	T 30	F	S	TOTAL	S	M

APRIL ATTENDANCE AND PAYMENT LOG CONTINUED

CHILD'S NAME	S	M	T	W 1	T 2	F 3	S 4	TOTAL	S 5	M 6	T 7	W 8	T 9	F 10	S 11	TOTAL	S 12	M 13	T 14	W 15	T 16	F 17	S 18	TOTAL	S 19	M 20	T 21	W 22	T 23	F 24	S 25	TOTAL	S 26	M 27	T 28	W 29	T 30	F	S	TOTAL	S	M

WEEKLY PAYMENT TOTALS

	FOOD PROGRAM INCOME RECVD	PARENT FEE INCOME RECVD	OTHER INCOME RECVD
APRIL INCOME			
BALANCE FORWARD			
TOTAL Y-T-D INCOME			

= APR TOTAL
= BALANCE FWD TOTAL
= TOTAL Y-T-D

Food Program Claim

Date Claim Sent _____

Date Check Received _____

MEAL COUNT TALLY

BREAKFASTS	
LUNCHES	
DINNERS	
SNACKS	

Put totals in year-end meal tally, page 95.

APRIL EXPENSE REPORT

DATE	PAYMENT TYPE cash, check #, cc #, debit	PURCHASED FROM	PURCHASE TOTAL	ADVERTISING	INSURANCE	INTEREST	LEGAL & PROFESSIONAL SERVICES	OFFICE EXPENSES (including internet & 2nd phone)	RENT OF BUSINESS PROPERTY	REPAIR & MAINTENANCE	SUPPLIES		MILES
		THIS MONTH'S TOTAL											
		BALANCE CARRIED FORWARD											
		YEAR-TO-DATE TOTAL											

APRIL EXPENSE REPORT

| DATE | PAYMENT TYPE
cash, check #, cc #, debit | PURCHASED FROM | PURCHASE TOTAL | TAXES & LICENSES | TRAVEL & ENTERTAINMENT | FOOD | TOYS | HOUSEHOLD ITEMS | CLEANING SUPPLIES | ACTIVITY EXPENSES | | | | MILES |
|---|---|---|---|---|---|---|---|---|---|---|---|---|---|---|
| | | | | | | | | | | | | | | |
| | | | | | | | | | | | | | | |
| | | | | | | | | | | | | | | |
| | | | | | | | | | | | | | | |
| | | | | | | | | | | | | | | |
| | | | | | | | | | | | | | | |
| | | | | | | | | | | | | | | |
| | | **THIS MONTH'S TOTAL** | | | | | | | | | | | | |
| | | **BALANCE CARRIED FORWARD** | | | | | | | | | | | | |
| | | **YEAR-TO-DATE TOTAL** | | | | | | | | | | | | |

See page 85 for an explanation of how to transfer expenses to your tax forms.
You may wish to relabel the columns to fit your business needs.

See page 6 for an explanation of the order in which we present the categories.

MAY 2026

* "No. Hours Open" refers to hours from when the first child arrived to when the last child left (not your advertised work hours).
** "Other Hours Worked" refers to hours spent on business activities in the home (cleaning, meal preparation, activity planning, and so on) when children are not present.

Hours Worked

Previous Total	
No. Hours Open*	
Other Hours Worked**	
Year-to-Date Total	

SUN	MON	TUE	WED	THU	FRI	SAT
APRIL 2026 / JUNE 2026					**1** Physical Fitness and Sports Month; May Day	**2**
3	**4** Fire Drill Day	**5** Cinco de Mayo; National Teacher Day	**6**	**7**	**8** Provider Appreciation Day	**9**
10 Mother's Day	**11**	**12**	**13** Severe Storm Drill Day	**14**	**15**	**16**
17	**18**	**19**	**20**	**21**	**22** Shavuot (Jewish)	**23**
24 Pentecost (Christian) / **31**	**25** Memorial Day; Hajj begins (Islamic); National Missing Children's Day	**26**	**27** Eid al-Adha (Islamic)	**28**	**29** Call your local R & R agency; update your service	**30**

MAY

Social and Emotional Learning

Glad, sad, mad are how we feel—
Our emotions are all real.

Recipes

Peachy Oatmeal Bake

- ¾ cup dry rolled oats (not quick)
- ½ cup low-fat milk
- 2 cups diced canned peaches, in light syrup (drained)
- 1 tablespoon maple syrup
- 1 teaspoon cinnamon
- 1½ cup sliced fresh peaches

1. Preheat oven to 400° F. Spray an 8-by-8-inch baking dish with nonstick cooking spray.
2. In a small bowl, combine oats, milk, peaches, maple syrup, and cinnamon. Stir.
3. Add oatmeal mixture to a baking dish. Bake for 30 minutes or until bubbling and golden brown. Remove from the oven and let sit for 5 minutes. Stir with a spoon to fluff. Serve each ½ cup portion with ¼ cup fresh peaches.

Yield: 6 servings
Meal Component: Grain

Pineapple Chicken

- 2 tablespoons low-sodium soy sauce
- 9¼ ounces diced cooked chicken breast
- ½ cup uncooked long-grain brown rice
- 2 tablespoons canola oil, divided
- 2 cups thinly sliced green onions
- 1 cup diced celery
- 2 cups canned crushed pineapple with juice, packed in juice or light syrup
- 4 teaspoons sugar
- 4 teaspoons cornstarch

1. In a plastic bag or medium bowl, stir together 2 tablespoons water, soy sauce, and salt and pepper to taste. Place chicken in bag, marinate in the refrigerator for 1 hour.
2. Combine brown rice and 1 cup water in a small pot. Heat to a rolling boil. Cover and reduce heat to low. Cook until water is absorbed, about 25 minutes.
3. Heat 1 tablespoon of oil on medium-high heat in a medium stockpot. Sauté green onions and celery for 3–5 minutes or until celery begins to cook but stays crunchy. Remove vegetables and set aside.
4. Add remaining 1 tablespoon oil to the pot. Add chicken, marinade, and pineapples with juice to pot. Bring to a boil, 5–7 minutes. Heat to 165° F or higher.
5. In a small bowl, whisk ¼ cup water together with sugar and cornstarch until smooth. Stir cornstarch mixture into the chicken and pineapple. Bring to a boil. Reduce heat and cook for 3–5 minutes or until sauce is nectar thick. Add 2 tablespoons of water if too thick.
6. Stir celery and green onions into pineapple chicken mixture and cook for 1 minute. Serve ⅔ cup pineapple chicken over ¼ cup cooked rice.

Yield: 6 servings
Meal Component: Meat/Meat Alternate, Grain, Fruit

Menu of the Month

Breakfast
Milk
Peachy Oatmeal Bake* (WG)

Morning Snack
Yogurt
Fresh Berries

Lunch
Milk
Pineapple Chicken* (WG)
Steamed Green Beans

Afternoon Snack
Mixed Nuts
Pea Pods

*Indicates recipes of the month.
(WG) Indicates whole grain.
Recipes adapted from the Institute of Childhood Nutrition.

Nutrition and Fitness Notes

As children learn their own body cues for hunger and fullness, encourage them to communicate when they are full and hungry and to demonstrate their understanding through mealtime serving and eating practices. Adults are responsible for providing nutritious, appetizing food in an appropriate setting; children can decide how much or even whether they eat.

The Experienced Provider

Social development describes how children learn to relate to others—interacting with adults and other children, building relationships, and developing friendships. Emotional development describes children's self-awareness and ability to control their feelings and expressions—awareness of feelings, sensitivity to others', and controlling one's own emotions and behavior. The social and emotional development domains are often coupled as one because they are so closely linked.

Activities for Children

Cleanup Time
Toddlers love to use brooms and mops. Find as many child-sized items as possible. Assign cleanup tasks after each activity (making sure you consider individual competency). Model your expectations and then be patient. Allow toddlers the opportunity to feel responsible and independent. Thank them for their efforts.

Happy Faces
Show the toddlers photographs of faces. Include a picture of each child. Spread them out so they can find photographs of themselves. Find a picture that looks happy. Ask all the children to make a happy face. Keep looking for happy face photographs. On another day, look for different kinds of expressions, such as excited, sad, and silly.

Facilitating Friendships
Cultivate peer acceptance by modeling inclusion, teaching children to respect differences through books, activities, and conversations. Facilitate friendships by scheduling and planning activities that encourage collaboration and interaction among all children. Address bullying or exclusion by intervening immediately and teaching empathy and problem-solving to the children.

Literacy Corner

When You Just Have to Roar! by Rachel Robertson
This book is about the ways one teacher helps her students practice managing emotions that make everyone happier.

I Like Myself! by Karen Beaumont
High on energy and imagination, this ode to self-esteem helps kids to appreciate everything about themselves—inside and out.

Serving sizes are for ages 3–5. Guidelines for the proper credit of food may vary in some states. Please check with the CACFP in your state for more information.

MAY ATTENDANCE AND PAYMENT LOG

To record drop-off and pickup times that vary, try using two lines per child.

CHILD'S NAME	S	M	T	W	T	F 1	S 2	TOTAL	S 3	M 4	T 5	W 6	T 7	F 8	S 9	TOTAL	S 10	M 11	T 12	W 13	T 14	F 15	S 16	TOTAL	S 17	M 18	T 19	W 20	T 21	F 22	S 23	TOTAL	S 24	M 25	T 26	W 27	T 28	F 29	S 30	TOTAL	S 31	M

MAY ATTENDANCE AND PAYMENT LOG CONTINUED

CHILD'S NAME	S	M	T	W	T	F 1	S 2	TOTAL	S 3	M 4	T 5	W 6	T 7	F 8	S 9	TOTAL	S 10	M 11	T 12	W 13	T 14	F 15	S 16	TOTAL	S 17	M 18	T 19	W 20	T 21	F 22	S 23	TOTAL	S 24	M 25	T 26	W 27	T 28	F 29	S 30	TOTAL	S 31	M

WEEKLY PAYMENT TOTALS

	FOOD PROGRAM INCOME RECVD	PARENT FEE INCOME RECVD	OTHER INCOME RECVD
MAY INCOME			
BALANCE FORWARD			
TOTAL Y-T-D INCOME			

= MAY TOTAL
= BALANCE FWD TOTAL
= TOTAL Y-T-D

Food Program Claim

Date Claim Sent _____

Date Check Received _____

MEAL COUNT TALLY

BREAKFASTS	
LUNCHES	
DINNERS	
SNACKS	

Put totals in year-end meal tally, page 95.

MAY EXPENSE REPORT

DATE	PAYMENT TYPE cash, check #, cc #, debit	PURCHASED FROM	PURCHASE TOTAL	ADVERTISING	INSURANCE	INTEREST	LEGAL & PROFESSIONAL SERVICES	OFFICE EXPENSES (including internet & 2nd phone)	RENT OF BUSINESS PROPERTY	REPAIR & MAINTENANCE	SUPPLIES		MILES
		THIS MONTH'S TOTAL											
		BALANCE CARRIED FORWARD											
		YEAR-TO-DATE TOTAL											

MAY EXPENSE REPORT

DATE	PAYMENT TYPE cash, check #, cc #, debit	PURCHASED FROM	PURCHASE TOTAL	TAXES & LICENSES	TRAVEL & ENTERTAINMENT	FOOD	TOYS	HOUSEHOLD ITEMS	CLEANING SUPPLIES	ACTIVITY EXPENSES			MILES
		THIS MONTH'S TOTAL											
		BALANCE CARRIED FORWARD											
		YEAR-TO-DATE TOTAL											

See page 85 for an explanation of how to transfer expenses to your tax forms. You may wish to relabel the columns to fit your business needs.

See page 6 for an explanation of the order in which we present the categories.

JUNE 2026

Hours Worked	
Previous Total	
No. Hours Open*	
Other Hours Worked**	
Year-to-Date Total	

* "No. Hours Open" refers to hours from when the first child arrived to when the last child left (not your advertised work hours).
** "Other Hours Worked" refers to hours spent on business activities in the home (cleaning, meal preparation, activity planning, and so on) when children are not present.

SUN	MON	TUE	WED	THU	FRI	SAT
	1 Fire Drill Day	**2**	**3**	**4**	**5**	**6**
7	**8**	**9**	**10** Severe Storm Drill Day	**11**	**12**	**13**
14 Flag Day	**15** 2026 2nd quarter estimated taxes due	**16**	**17** Islamic New Year	**18**	**19** Juneteenth	**20**
21 Father's Day Summer begins	**22**	**23**	**24**	**25**	**26** Ashura (Islamic)	**27**
28	**29**	**30** Call your local R & R agency; update your service				

Replenish your stock of *Family Child Care Business Receipt Books, Inventory-Keepers,* and *Mileage-Keepers.*

JUNE

Let's Go Outside

Go outside and feel the breeze—
See the sky, flowers, and trees!

Recipes

Egg and Broccoli Scramble

6 eggs
½ teaspoon garlic powder
1 tablespoon grated parmesan cheese
1¾ cups chopped frozen broccoli, thawed and drained

1. In a medium bowl, combine eggs, 1 tablespoon water, garlic powder, parmesan cheese, and salt and pepper to taste. Whisk to mix.
2. Spray a small nonstick skillet with nonstick cooking spray. Heat skillet on medium-high heat. Sauté thawed broccoli for 3–5 minutes or until broccoli begins to turn brown on the tips of the crowns.
3. Add egg mixture. Stir eggs and broccoli, constantly removing any egg sticking to the bottom of the pan.

Yield: 6 servings, ⅓ cup each
Meal Component: Meat/Meat Alternate

Very Berry Parfaits

5¾ cups frozen berry medley (unsweetened), thawed and drained
1½ cups low-fat vanilla yogurt
¾ cups granola (optional)

1. In clear 10-ounce plastic cups, layer parfait ingredients in the following order: ½ cup fruit, ¼ cup yogurt, and 2 tablespoons granola (optional).

Yield: 6 servings
Meal Component: Meat/Meat Alternate, Fruit

Menu of the Month

Breakfast
Milk
Egg and Broccoli Scramble*
Bananas

Morning Snack
Water
Very Berry Parfaits*

Lunch
Milk
Whole Wheat Spaghetti with Marinara Sauce (WG)
Turkey Meatballs
Green Beans
Mango Chunks

Afternoon Snack
Whole Grain Crackers (WG)
String Cheese

*Indicates recipes of the month.
(WG) Indicates whole grain.
Recipes adapted from the Institute of Childhood Nutrition.

Nutrition and Fitness Notes

Provide dense shade in outdoor play areas to extend the time of day when outside play is comfortable and to prevent overexposure to the sun's ultraviolet rays. Plan for a variety of activities. Tricycle paths, grassy areas for running and playing, and areas for digging all contribute to a diverse outdoor environment and promote fun physical activity.

The Experienced Provider

We often think of rich moments as those that feel "special" for some reason. Yet mundane moments are meaningful. If we don't reframe the mundane as rich, we are suggesting that a child's day holds little for us to be interested in. When we come to see that these everyday moments are filled with endless possibility and significance, we are left to wonder: How do we respond? What is a concrete way to honor this richness? How do we develop our eye for the unseen features and perspectives of life?

Activities for Children

Nature Walks

Take the toddlers on nature walks throughout the year. Look at flowers, trees, and insects. Start collections that include pine cones, shells, rocks, and bugs so toddlers can see similarities and patterns. Play a matching game using two leaves from each tree. Go outside after it rains and look at a puddle. Draw a line around the puddle with chalk or a stick. Watch the puddle throughout the day as it dries.

Collage Treasure Hunt

Go on a treasure hunt outside to find things that can be used in a collage, such as sticks and leaves, flowers to be pressed, pebbles, and shells (avoid feathers, as in the United States they are often illegal to collect). You can also add scraps of paper, buttons, pieces of cloth, and ribbons. Use heavy cardboard or wood as backing. Have the children lay out the materials in a design on the backing. Supervise the children while they glue the items on the backing or save the materials to be reused and redesigned repeatedly.

In Our Community

When you regularly take walks in your neighborhood, you can get to know the people on the streets and the businesses around you. Consider these questions to support this engagement with the wider community: (1) How do children view community and define community? (2) How would children change the community if given the chance? (3) How do children use their voices to speak up for social justice? and (4) How might children build connections and their sense of responsibility for community?

Literacy Corner

Outdoor Time by Elizabeth Verdick
Join a group of toddlers as they dress for outdoors; find balls, pails, binoculars, and treasures; and head outside to shout, run, play, and explore.

Noah Chases the Wind by Michelle Worthington
Noah Chases the Wind is a colorful and magical adventure that celebrates the inquisitive nature of all children, as well as the unique characteristics of children on the autism spectrum.

JUNE ATTENDANCE AND PAYMENT LOG

To record drop-off and pickup times that vary, try using two lines per child.

CHILD'S NAME	S 1	M 2	T 3	W 4	T 5	F 6	S	TOTAL	S 7	M 8	T 9	W 10	T 11	F 12	S 13	TOTAL	S 14	M 15	T 16	W 17	T 18	F 19	S 20	TOTAL	S 21	M 22	T 23	W 24	T 25	F 26	S 27	TOTAL	S 28	M 29	T 30	W	T	F	S	TOTAL	S	M

JUNE ATTENDANCE AND PAYMENT LOG CONTINUED

CHILD'S NAME	S 1	M 2	T 3	W 4	T 5	F 6	S	TOTAL	S 7	M 8	T 9	W 10	T 11	F 12	S 13	TOTAL	S 14	M 15	T 16	W 17	T 18	F 19	S 20	TOTAL	S 21	M 22	T 23	W 24	T 25	F 26	S 27	TOTAL	S 28	M 29	T 30	W	T	F	S	TOTAL	S	M

WEEKLY PAYMENT TOTALS

	FOOD PROGRAM INCOME RECVD	PARENT FEE INCOME RECVD	OTHER INCOME RECVD			
JUNE INCOME				=	JUN TOTAL	
BALANCE FORWARD				=	BALANCE FWD TOTAL	
TOTAL Y-T-D INCOME				=	TOTAL Y-T-D	

Food Program Claim

Date Claim Sent _____

Date Check Received _____

MEAL COUNT TALLY	
BREAKFASTS	
LUNCHES	
DINNERS	
SNACKS	

Put totals in year-end meal tally, page 95.

JUNE EXPENSE REPORT

DATE	PAYMENT TYPE cash, check #, cc #, debit	PURCHASED FROM	PURCHASE TOTAL	ADVERTISING	INSURANCE	INTEREST	LEGAL & PROFESSIONAL SERVICES	OFFICE EXPENSES (including internet & 2nd phone)	RENT OF BUSINESS PROPERTY	REPAIR & MAINTENANCE	SUPPLIES		MILES
		THIS MONTH'S TOTAL											
		BALANCE CARRIED FORWARD											
		YEAR-TO-DATE TOTAL											

JUNE EXPENSE REPORT

DATE	PAYMENT TYPE cash, check #, cc #, debit	PURCHASED FROM	PURCHASE TOTAL	TAXES & LICENSES	TRAVEL & ENTERTAINMENT	FOOD	TOYS	HOUSEHOLD ITEMS	CLEANING SUPPLIES	ACTIVITY EXPENSES			MILES
		THIS MONTH'S TOTAL											
		BALANCE CARRIED FORWARD											
		YEAR-TO-DATE TOTAL											

See page 85 for an explanation of how to transfer expenses to your tax forms. You may wish to relabel the columns to fit your business needs.

See page 6 for an explanation of the order in which we present the categories.

JULY 2026

	Hours Worked
Previous Total	
No. Hours Open*	
Other Hours Worked**	
Year-to-Date Total	

* "No. Hours Open" refers to hours from when the first child arrived to when the last child left (not your advertised work hours).
** "Other Hours Worked" refers to hours spent on business activities in the home (cleaning, meal preparation, activity planning, and so on) when children are not present.

SUN	MON	TUE	WED	THU	FRI	SAT
			1	2	3	4 Independence Day
5	6 Fire Drill Day	7	8 Severe Storm Drill Day	9	10	11
12	13	14	15	16	17	18
19	20	21	22	23 Tishah B'Av (Jewish)	24	25
26 Parents' Day	27	28	29	30	31 Call your local R & R agency; update your service	

JULY

Make New Friends
At the playground, library, beach, or fair—
New friends might be anywhere!

Recipes

Cheesy Drop Biscuits

½ cup enriched all-purpose flour
½ cup whole wheat pastry flour
1 teaspoon baking powder
1 tablespoon sugar
⅛ teaspoon salt
2 teaspoons trans fat-free margarine, chilled
½ cup nonfat plain Greek yogurt
¼ cup reduced-fat cheddar cheese, shredded
¼ cup fat-free milk

1. Preheat oven to 400° F. Line baking sheet with parchment paper and spray with nonstick cooking spray.
2. In a small bowl, combine all-purpose flour, pastry flour, baking powder, sugar, and salt. Mix.
3. Using a fork or pastry cutter, mash margarine into dry ingredients. Add yogurt and mash into dry ingredients until the flour turns into fine crumbs.
4. Using the fork or pastry cutter, lightly mash cheese into the dough. Add milk. Stir until ingredients are well blended. Dough will be very sticky.
5. Using a ¼ cup measuring cup, drop dough onto baking sheet. Lightly spray the top of biscuits with nonstick cooking spray. Bake biscuits for 13–15 minutes or until golden brown.

Yield: 6 servings, 1 biscuit each
Meal Component: Grain

Chicken Curry Casserole

1 cup long-grain brown rice
1 tablespoon canola oil
¼ cup low-sodium chicken broth
¾ cup diced fresh celery
1 cup diced fresh onions
1¼ cups shredded fresh carrots
1½ teaspoon curry powder
1 teaspoon garlic powder
½ cup low-fat plain yogurt
12 ounces cooked fajita chicken strips, diced

Serving sizes are for ages 3–5. Guidelines for the proper credit of food may vary in some states. Please check with the CACFP in your state for more information.

Menu of the Month

Breakfast
Milk
Cheesy Drop Biscuits* (WG)
Pitted Cherries

Morning Snack
Water
Carrot and Celery Sticks
Peanut Butter

Lunch
Milk
Chicken Curry Casserole* (WG)
Strawberries

Afternoon Snack
Water
Graham Crackers
100% Apple Juice

*Indicates recipes of the month.
(WG) Indicates whole grain.
Recipes adapted from the Institute of Childhood Nutrition.

1. Preheat oven to 400° F. Combine brown rice and 2½ cups water in large pot and bring to a boil. Turn heat down to low. Cover and cook until water is absorbed, about 30 to 40 minutes. Fluff with a fork. Set aside.
2. In a large pan, heat canola oil and chicken broth over medium heat for 2 to 3 minutes. Add celery, onions, and carrots. Cook an additional 5 to 7 minutes or until vegetables are tender.
3. In a large mixing bowl, combine curry powder, garlic powder, yogurt, and salt and pepper to taste. Add vegetables, brown rice, and chicken. Mix well.
4. Pour mixture into a 9-by-9-inch nonstick baking pan. Bake uncovered for 15 minutes. Heat to an internal temperature of 165° F.

Yield: 6 servings
Meal Component: Grain, Meat/Meat Alternate, Vegetable

Nutrition and Fitness Notes

Mealtime and snacktime activities provide opportunities to show children how to share food appropriately. Show children how to cut a sandwich in half before taking a bite, how to pour beverages from a small pitcher into individual cups, and how to use tongs or a napkin to remove a cracker or cookie from a serving tray.

The Experienced Provider

To a great extent, social development becomes a crucial factor in determining children's ability to be successful in school and life. Children who exhibit appropriate social development can make friends and interact positively with other children and adults. In family child care environments, where continuity of care is so important, children can develop a sense of trust and security. Those are the very characteristics that allow them to develop confidence.

Activities for Children

Group Activities and Playdates
Ensuring your daily activity schedule includes regular opportunities for children to engage in group activities and social interactions will improve their ability to relate to others and eventually build friendships. Encouraging the families in your program to consider pairing up for the children to gather on playdates provides further opportunities to practice social connections.

My New Friends Book
At the beginning of the year, ask each child to bring in a photograph, or take a picture of each child. Glue each picture to a piece of paper and ask the children to tell you a story about themselves. Put all the pictures together to make a book, *My New Friends*. Each night a different child can take the book home and introduce his family to new school friends.

Changing the Rules
All young children benefit when they come to understand that everyone is not the same and that's okay. For example, demonstrating to children how to change the rules of a game to accommodate everyone present offers an invaluable teaching opportunity. You may be pleasantly surprised to see how children accommodate one another when given the opportunity.

Literacy Corner

Bree Finds a Friend by Mike Huber
Bree is digging for worms, but she unearths something even better than she expected—a new friend!

My Three Best Friends and Me, Zulay by Cari Best
When their teacher asks her students what activity they want to do on Field Day, Zulay, who is blind, surprises everyone when she says she wants to run a race.

JULY ATTENDANCE AND PAYMENT LOG

To record drop-off and pickup times that vary, try using two lines per child.

CHILD'S NAME	S	M	T	W	T	F	S	TOTAL	S	M	T	W	T	F	S	TOTAL	S	M	T	W	T	F	S	TOTAL	S	M	T	W	T	F	S	TOTAL	S	M	T	W	T	F	S	TOTAL	S	M
				1	2	3	4		5	6	7	8	9	10	11		12	13	14	15	16	17	18		19	20	21	22	23	24	25		26	27	28	29	30	31				

JULY ATTENDANCE AND PAYMENT LOG CONTINUED

CHILD'S NAME	S	M	T	W	T	F	S	TOTAL	S	M	T	W	T	F	S	TOTAL	S	M	T	W	T	F	S	TOTAL	S	M	T	W	T	F	S	TOTAL	S	M	T	W	T	F	S	TOTAL	S	M
			1	2	3	4			5	6	7	8	9	10	11		12	13	14	15	16	17	18		19	20	21	22	23	24	25		26	27	28	29	30	31				

WEEKLY PAYMENT TOTALS

	FOOD PROGRAM INCOME RECVD	PARENT FEE INCOME RECVD	OTHER INCOME RECVD			
JULY INCOME				=	JUL TOTAL	
BALANCE FORWARD				=	BALANCE FWD TOTAL	
TOTAL Y-T-D INCOME				=	TOTAL Y-T-D	

Food Program Claim

Date Claim Sent _____

Date Check Received _____

MEAL COUNT TALLY

BREAKFASTS	
LUNCHES	
DINNERS	
SNACKS	

Put totals in year-end meal tally, page 95.

JULY EXPENSE REPORT

DATE	PAYMENT TYPE cash, check #, cc #, debit	PURCHASED FROM	PURCHASE TOTAL	ADVERTISING	INSURANCE	INTEREST	LEGAL & PROFESSIONAL SERVICES	OFFICE EXPENSES (including internet & 2nd phone)	RENT OF BUSINESS PROPERTY	REPAIR & MAINTENANCE	SUPPLIES		MILES
		THIS MONTH'S TOTAL											
		BALANCE CARRIED FORWARD											
		YEAR-TO-DATE TOTAL											

JULY EXPENSE REPORT

DATE	PAYMENT TYPE cash, check #, cc #, debit	PURCHASED FROM	PURCHASE TOTAL	TAXES & LICENSES	TRAVEL & ENTERTAINMENT	FOOD	TOYS	HOUSEHOLD ITEMS	CLEANING SUPPLIES	ACTIVITY EXPENSES			MILES
			THIS MONTH'S TOTAL										
			BALANCE CARRIED FORWARD										
			YEAR-TO-DATE TOTAL										

See page 85 for an explanation of how to transfer expenses to your tax forms. You may wish to relabel the columns to fit your business needs.

See page 6 for an explanation of the order in which we present the categories.

AUGUST 2026

	Hours Worked
Previous Total	
No. Hours Open*	
Other Hours Worked**	
Year-to-Date Total	

* "No. Hours Open" refers to hours from when the first child arrived to when the last child left (not your advertised work hours).

** "Other Hours Worked" refers to hours spent on business activities in the home (cleaning, meal preparation, activity planning, and so on) when children are not present.

SUN	MON	TUE	WED	THU	FRI	SAT
JULY 2026 / SEPTEMBER 2026						**1**
2 Friendship Day	**3** Fire Drill Day	**4**	**5**	**6**	**7**	**8**
9	**10**	**11**	**12** Severe Storm Drill Day	**13**	**14**	**15**
16	**17**	**18**	**19**	**20**	**21**	**22**
23	**24**	**25**	**26** Women's Equality Day / Mawlid al-Nabi (Islamic)	**27**	**28**	**29**
30	**31** Call your local R & R agency; update your service					

AUGUST

Growing Gardens
With water and seeds, shovel and hoe,
We love to help our garden grow!

Recipes

Parmesan Chicken Tenders

13½ ounces chicken tenders (at least 6 tenders)
3 tablespoons Italian dressing
2 tablespoons grated parmesan cheese
2 tablespoons whole wheat seasoned breadcrumbs
2 tablespoons plain enriched panko breadcrumbs

1. Place chicken tenders and Italian dressing in a bowl. Cover. Marinate in the refrigerator for 2–6 hours or overnight.
2. Preheat oven to 400° F. Place a baking rack on top of a baking sheet. Spray rack with nonstick cooking spray.
3. In a small bowl, combine parmesan cheese and breadcrumbs. Mix.
4. Remove chicken tenders from dressing. Discard any remaining Italian dressing. Coat tenders with parmesan breading. Place on prepared baking rack. Bake for 20 minutes. Heat to an internal temperature of 165° F.

Yield: 6 servings, one tender each
Meal Component: Meat/Meat Alternate

Cottage Cheese and Fruit Bowls

1 cup peeled and sliced fresh kiwi
1 cup fresh whole blueberries
1 cup sliced fresh strawberries
¾ cup low-fat cottage cheese
6 tablespoons granola (optional)

1. Wash fruit before slicing. Place kiwi, blueberries, and strawberries in a small bowl. Toss to combine.
2. Place ½ cup fruit in a bowl. Top with 2 tablespoons cottage cheese and 1 tablespoon granola (optional).

Yield: 6 servings, 1 bowl each
Meal Component: Fruit, Meat/Meat Alternate

Serving sizes are for ages 3–5. Guidelines for the proper credit of food may vary in some states. Please check with the CACFP in your state for more information.

Menu of the Month

Breakfast
Milk
Whole Grain Cereal (WG)
Raspberries

Morning Snack
Water
Hard-Boiled Egg
Kohlrabi Chunks

Lunch
Milk
Chicken Parmesan Tenders*
Whole Wheat Bun (WG)
Nectarines
Spinach Salad

Afternoon Snack
Cottage Cheese and Fruit Bowls*

*Indicates recipes of the month.
(WG) Indicates whole grain.
Recipes adapted from the Institute of Childhood Nutrition.

Nutrition and Fitness Notes

Children must have water available to them throughout the day, including during outside playtime and on field trips. Children lose fluid from their bodies throughout the day but especially when participating in vigorous play (such as running and jumping) and during warm weather. They can become dehydrated very quickly, leading to a potentially dangerous health condition.

The Experienced Provider

Children learn through their senses. Incorporate activities that allow young children the opportunity to use all their senses: seeing, hearing, touching, tasting, and smelling. Cooking and gardening are wonderful activities to stimulate all senses.

Activities for Children

Sensory Dirt
Fill a small tub with an inch of soil or sand, or go outside to the sandbox or garden. Provide large wooden spoons or shovels and assorted sizes of plastic containers or measuring cups. Let the children feel the soil or sand. Encourage them to pick some up and let it fall back into the container. Ask them to describe how the material feels. Even young infants will enjoy this sensory activity.

Garden Field Trip
A visit to a garden center can be highly interesting and educational for young children. And it's free! Select a garden center that welcomes educational visits. Some stores may open early for special visits, and others may have special celebrations for children, such as pumpkin festivals. Be sure to let the store know what types of items you want the children to see. They may be able to provide a guide. It is helpful for children to have a goal in mind when they go on a field trip, such as choosing a plant to purchase or answering a question about caring for a plant.

Children's Contributions
Children naturally want to contribute to the well-being of others and the community. When children help, they develop skills and competencies while growing their self-esteem and their sense of belonging. Throughout human history children have been appreciated for helping in their family and kinship networks. Most Indigenous groups have long believed that children would not learn the skills or dispositions needed for the community to survive if they weren't given responsibilities early in their lives. In modern times, children are less often asked to participate in the real work of the community, which undermines their natural desire to participate as well as their sense of belonging and helpfulness.

Literacy Corner

The Young Garden King by Terrius Bruce
In a little town, young Imhotep noticed there weren't any places to get yummy, fresh fruits and veggies! So, he had a big idea: What if he could grow them right in his backyard?

Bugs! Bugs! Bugs! by Bob Barner
Pretty ladybugs, fluttering butterflies, creepy daddy longlegs, and roly-poly bugs are some of the familiar creatures featured in this whimsically illustrated insect album.

AUGUST ATTENDANCE AND PAYMENT LOG

To record drop-off and pickup times that vary, try using two lines per child.

CHILD'S NAME	S 1	M	T	W	T	F	S	TOTAL	S 2	M 3	T 4	W 5	T 6	F 7	S 8	TOTAL	S 9	M 10	T 11	W 12	T 13	F 14	S 15	TOTAL	S 16	M 17	T 18	W 19	T 20	F 21	S 22	TOTAL	S 23	M 24	T 25	W 26	T 27	F 28	S 29	TOTAL	S 30	M 31

AUGUST ATTENDANCE AND PAYMENT LOG CONTINUED

CHILD'S NAME	S	M	T	W	T	F	S 1	TOTAL	S 2	M 3	T 4	W 5	T 6	F 7	S 8	TOTAL	S 9	M 10	T 11	W 12	T 13	F 14	S 15	TOTAL	S 16	M 17	T 18	W 19	T 20	F 21	S 22	TOTAL	S 23	M 24	T 25	W 26	T 27	F 28	S 29	TOTAL	S 30	M 31
WEEKLY PAYMENT TOTALS																																										

	FOOD PROGRAM INCOME RECVD	PARENT FEE INCOME RECVD	OTHER INCOME RECVD			
AUGUST INCOME				=	AUG TOTAL	
BALANCE FORWARD				=	BALANCE FWD TOTAL	
TOTAL Y-T-D INCOME				=	TOTAL Y-T-D	

Food Program Claim

Date Claim Sent _____

Date Check Received _____

MEAL COUNT TALLY

BREAKFASTS	
LUNCHES	
DINNERS	
SNACKS	

Put totals in year-end meal tally, page 95.

AUGUST EXPENSE REPORT

DATE	PAYMENT TYPE cash, check #, cc #, debit	PURCHASED FROM	PURCHASE TOTAL	ADVERTISING	INSURANCE	INTEREST	LEGAL & PROFESSIONAL SERVICES	OFFICE EXPENSES (including internet & 2nd phone)	RENT OF BUSINESS PROPERTY	REPAIR & MAINTENANCE	SUPPLIES		MILES
		THIS MONTH'S TOTAL											
		BALANCE CARRIED FORWARD											
		YEAR-TO-DATE TOTAL											

AUGUST EXPENSE REPORT

DATE	PAYMENT TYPE cash, check #, cc #, debit	PURCHASED FROM	PURCHASE TOTAL	TAXES & LICENSES	TRAVEL & ENTERTAINMENT	FOOD	TOYS	HOUSEHOLD ITEMS	CLEANING SUPPLIES	ACTIVITY EXPENSES			MILES
		THIS MONTH'S TOTAL											
		BALANCE CARRIED FORWARD											
		YEAR-TO-DATE TOTAL											

See page 85 for an explanation of how to transfer expenses to your tax forms.
You may wish to relabel the columns to fit your business needs.

See page 6 for an explanation of the order in which we present the categories.

SEPTEMBER 2026

Hours Worked
Previous Total	
No. Hours Open*	
Other Hours Worked**	
Year-to-Date Total	

* "No. Hours Open" refers to hours from when the first child arrived to when the last child left (not your advertised work hours).
** "Other Hours Worked" refers to hours spent on business activities in the home (cleaning, meal preparation, activity planning, and so on) when children are not present.

SUN	MON	TUE	WED	THU	FRI	SAT
		1	**2**	**3**	**4**	**5**
	The Redleaf Calendar-Keeper™ 2027 is available now!					
6	**7** Labor Day / Fire Drill Day	**8**	**9** Severe Storm Drill Day	**10**	**11** Patriot Day	**12** Rosh Hashanah (Jewish)
13 Grandparents' Day	**14**	**15** Start of National Hispanic Heritage Month / 2026 3rd quarter estimated taxes due	**16**	**17** Constitution Day	**18**	**19**
20	**21** Yom Kippur (Jewish)	**22** Autumn begins / Change your smoke alarm and carbon monoxide filter batteries	**23**	**24**	**25** Native American Day	**26** Sukkot begins (Jewish)
27	**28**	**29**	**30** Call your local R & R agency; update your service			

SEPTEMBER

We Are Healthy
We play outside and eat good food
It helps our bodies, health, and mood!

Recipes

Baked Cod Olé

3 tablespoons lime juice
½ teaspoon olive oil
1¼ cups fresh tomatoes, diced
1¼ cups fresh onions, diced
2 tablespoons cilantro, chopped
13½ ounces codfish fillets, fresh or frozen (6 pieces, 2¼ ounce each)

1. To make dressing: In a small bowl, whisk together lime juice, olive oil, and salt and pepper to taste.
2. To make salsa: In a medium bowl, combine tomatoes, onions, and cilantro. Add dressing and toss.
3. Preheat oven to 400° F. Coat baking sheet with nonstick cooking spray. Place fish portions on a baking sheet with about 1 inch of space separating each piece.
4. Top each piece of fish with ⅓ cup salsa. Roast for 12–15 minutes. When done, fish will flake easily with a fork. Heat to an internal temperature of 155° F. Serve 1 fillet topped with ⅓ cup salsa.

Yield: 6 servings
Meal Component: Meat/Meat Alternate, Vegetable

Baked Tofu Bites

1 pound 4 ounces firm tofu, rinsed, drained, and cut into ½-inch cubes
2 tablespoons hoisin sauce
2 tablespoons reduced-sodium soy sauce
½ cup whole wheat flour
¼ cup whole grain cornmeal
¼ teaspoon ground mustard
¼ teaspoon garlic powder

Serving sizes are for ages 3–5. Guidelines for the proper credit of food may vary in some states. Please check with the CACFP in your state for more information.

Menu of the Month

Breakfast
Milk
Whole Grain Grits (WG)
Baked Apples

Morning Snack
Water
Almonds
Raisins

Lunch
Milk
Baked Cod Olé*
Watermelon
Quinoa (WG)

Afternoon Snack
Baked Tofu Bites*

*Indicates recipes of the month.
(WG) Indicates whole grain.
Recipes adapted from the Institute of Childhood Nutrition.

1. To make marinade: In a 1-gallon plastic bag, combine hoisin sauce, soy sauce, and 1 tablespoon water. Add tofu cubes to marinade. Seal the bag tightly. Lightly toss tofu by turning the bag over repeatedly on a flat surface to prevent tofu from breaking apart. Marinate in the refrigerator for 1 hour. Turn bag over every 15 minutes.
2. In a separate 1-gallon plastic bag, combine whole wheat flour, cornmeal, dry mustard, and garlic powder. Shake to mix.
3. Preheat oven to 400° F. Lightly spray a baking sheet with nonstick cooking spray.
4. Remove tofu from marinade a few cubes at a time. Place tofu cubes in the bag with the flour-cornmeal mixture. Carefully turn the bag over to coat the tofu with breading. Remove coated tofu cubes and place on baking sheet in a single layer. Repeat until all tofu cubes are coated. Discard any remaining marinade.
5. Bake for 15 minutes or until tofu is lightly crisp.

Yield: 6 servings, ¾ cup each
Meal Component: Meat/Meat Alternate, Grain

Nutrition and Fitness Notes

Children's growth and development depends on having balanced meals and snacks rich in essential nutrients. Family child care educators can achieve this goal by simply following their state or federal food program guidelines, which are often aligned with requirements from the US Department of Agriculture (USDA).

The Experienced Provider

Make sure that any equipment, including cribs or playpens, is appropriate for the weight and mobility of the child. Check recall lists regularly. Always read labels and instructions carefully. Because family child care includes multiage groups, it is not uncommon for younger children to want to play with and do everything the older children do.

Activities for Children

Hand Washing

Discuss when it is important to wash hands: before and after eating, after activities, when coming in from outside. Let older children demonstrate their skills by showing infants how to wash their hands. If you do not use paper towels, have a designated hand towel for each child in your program. Sing "Twinkle, Twinkle Little Star" while infants wash their hands. This will encourage them to continue washing for an appropriate duration.

Stopping Germs

Teach children that eating utensils (forks and spoons) are for individual use—they should not put their utensils in a serving bowl. Provide individual cups or reusable water bottles for drinking, and help children pour water for themselves throughout the day. Be sure to clean and sanitize water bottles each day.

Inclusive Programming

When accepting children with diagnosed disabilities and other support needs, the same basic principles of quality family child care remain the same. This includes maintaining both an environment and a daily schedule that allows each child to actively participate and, even more importantly, to benefit as a result of their participation.

Literacy Corner

Those Mean Nasty Dirty Downright Disgusting but . . . Invisible Germs by Judith Anne Rice
Children will be delighted by the imaginative, full-color illustrations of the germs. Bilingual English/Spanish.

Eating the Alphabet by Lois Ehlert
While teaching upper- and lowercase letters to preschoolers, Ehlert introduces fruits and vegetables from around the world.

SEPTEMBER ATTENDANCE AND PAYMENT LOG

To record drop-off and pickup times that vary, try using two lines per child.

CHILD'S NAME	S	M 1	T 2	W 3	T 4	F 5	S 5	TOTAL	S 6	M 7	T 8	W 9	T 10	F 11	S 12	TOTAL	S 13	M 14	T 15	W 16	T 17	F 18	S 19	TOTAL	S 20	M 21	T 22	W 23	T 24	F 25	S 26	TOTAL	S 27	M 28	T 29	W 30	T	F	S	TOTAL	S	M

SEPTEMBER ATTENDANCE AND PAYMENT LOG CONTINUED

CHILD'S NAME	S	M T W T F S 1 2 3 4 5	TOTAL	S M T W T F S 6 7 8 9 10 11 12	TOTAL	S M T W T F S 13 14 15 16 17 18 19	TOTAL	S M T W T F S 20 21 22 23 24 25 26	TOTAL	S M T W T F S 27 28 29 30	TOTAL	S M

WEEKLY PAYMENT TOTALS

	FOOD PROGRAM INCOME RECVD	PARENT FEE INCOME RECVD	OTHER INCOME RECVD			
SEPTEMBER INCOME				=	SEPT TOTAL	
BALANCE FORWARD				=	BALANCE FWD TOTAL	
TOTAL Y-T-D INCOME				=	TOTAL Y-T-D	

Food Program Claim

Date Claim Sent _____

Date Check Received _____

MEAL COUNT TALLY

BREAKFASTS	
LUNCHES	
DINNERS	
SNACKS	

Put totals in year-end meal tally, page 95.

SEPTEMBER EXPENSE REPORT

DATE	PAYMENT TYPE cash, check #, cc #, debit	PURCHASED FROM	PURCHASE TOTAL	ADVERTISING	INSURANCE	INTEREST	LEGAL & PROFESSIONAL SERVICES	OFFICE EXPENSES (including internet & 2nd phone)	RENT OF BUSINESS PROPERTY	REPAIR & MAINTENANCE	SUPPLIES		MILES
		THIS MONTH'S TOTAL											
		BALANCE CARRIED FORWARD											
		YEAR-TO-DATE TOTAL											

SEPTEMBER EXPENSE REPORT

DATE	PAYMENT TYPE cash, check #, cc #, debit	PURCHASED FROM	PURCHASE TOTAL	TAXES & LICENSES	TRAVEL & ENTERTAINMENT	FOOD	TOYS	HOUSEHOLD ITEMS	CLEANING SUPPLIES	ACTIVITY EXPENSES			MILES
		THIS MONTH'S TOTAL											
		BALANCE CARRIED FORWARD											
		YEAR-TO-DATE TOTAL											

See page 85 for an explanation of how to transfer expenses to your tax forms. You may wish to relabel the columns to fit your business needs.

See page 6 for an explanation of the order in which we present the categories.

OCTOBER 2026

Hours Worked
- Previous Total
- No. Hours Open*
- Other Hours Worked**
- Year-to-Date Total

* "No. Hours Open" refers to hours from when the first child arrived to when the last child left (not your advertised work hours).

** "Other Hours Worked" refers to hours spent on business activities in the home (cleaning, meal preparation, activity planning, and so on) when children are not present.

SUN	MON	TUE	WED	THU	FRI	SAT
SEPTEMBER 2026	NOVEMBER 2026			1 National Bullying Prevention Month; Breast Cancer Awareness Month	2 Sukkot ends (Jewish)	3
4	5 Child Health Day; Fire Drill Day	6	7	8	9	10
11	12 Columbus Day; Indigenous Peoples' Day	13	14 Severe Storm Drill Day	15 End of National Hispanic Heritage Month	16	17
18	19	20	21	22	23	24
25	26	27	28	29	30 Call your local R & R agency; update your service	31 Halloween

Time Flies
When You're Running a Business!

Now is the perfect time to place your order for the business essentials you'll need next year. Order now and you'll be ready to go for 2026.

The Redleaf Calendar-Keeper™ 2027
A Record-Keeping System for Family Child Care Professionals

Year after year, *The Redleaf Calendar-Keeper* is the most reliable organizational resource for family child care professionals. Continue to save time and money by ordering your 2027 edition now!

#100027-CK26 $21.95

Family Child Care Business Receipt Book

Improve your record keeping with receipts designed specifically for family child care. Three books, each with 50 carbonless duplicate sets of receipts, are included.

#106101-CK26 $15.95

Family Child Care Mileage-Keeper

Record business trips, repairs, tolls, parking, and other car expenses. Forms are included for one year's worth of records.

#104101-CK26 $7.95

Family Child Care Inventory-Keeper

Track furniture, appliances, and other property used in your business for depreciation and insurance purposes.

#107001-CK26 $14.95

Family Child Care Sharing in the Caring
Agreement Packet for Parents and Providers

Establish a clear understanding with parents from the start. This packet contains five copies of a formal two-part agreement form as well as instructions for how to complete contract terms for rates, holidays, vacations, payment dates, and illnesses.

#101301-CK26 $9.95
Forms only (pack of five) #101601-CK26 $8.95

See pages 5 and 66 for additional resources.

Redleaf Press® 10 Yorkton Court, St. Paul, MN 55117-1065

Call 800-423-8309 • Fax 800-641-0115 • www.redleafpress.org

Name _____

Address _____ Apt. _____

City _____

State [ ]   Zip Code [ ][ ][ ][ ][ ]-[ ][ ][ ][ ]   CK26

Daytime phone (_____) _____   E-mail _____

QTY	ITEM #	TITLE	CATALOG PRICE	AMOUNT

Shipping & Handling Charges

Order Size . . . . Add
$0 to $49.99 . . . . $7.95
$50.00 to $99.99 . . . . . $10.95
$100.00 to $149.99 . . . $13.95
$150.00 or more . . . . . 10% of net order

SUBTOTAL
Shipping/Handling
Your applicable state* and county sales TAX
TOTAL

Alaska, Hawaii, and APO orders are shipped by priority mail; standard rates apply. Foreign orders are shipped by U.S. Postal Service. Call for pricing.

*We currently collect sales tax in these states: IL, IN, MA, MD, MI, MN, MO, NC, OK, PA, TN, WI.

Payment: (U.S. funds only. Sorry, we cannot accept COD orders.)

[ ] Check or money order enclosed. DO NOT send cash.

Charge to credit card: [ ] Visa [ ] MC [ ] Discover [ ] American Express

[ ][ ][ ][ ] [ ][ ][ ][ ] [ ][ ][ ][ ] [ ][ ][ ][ ]   Expiration Date [ ][ ] / [ ][ ]
                                                                Month   Year

[ ][ ][ ] CVN (3-digit code on the back of card)

Cardholder signature (required) _____

Prices subject to change without notice.

Tom Copeland Resources

Tom Copeland, JD, is a licensed attorney, leading tax specialist, and award-winning advocate for the business of family child care.

NEW! Family Child Care 2025 Tax Workbook and Organizer
Tom Copeland is the nation's leading expert on the business of family child care. Updated annually, this is the most comprehensive resource available. This edition contains guidance on navigating new tax laws, tips to help save money, and tools that take the guesswork out of family child care business taxes. Softbound, 264 pgs.

#100825-CK26 $21.95

NEW! Family Child Care 2025 Tax Companion
The *Tax Companion* is a comprehensive tool that will help tax preparers understand the rules that affect family child care businesses. It also includes information on the new tax laws that relate to depreciation. Using this resource will increase your confidence in the tax professionals who prepare your return, help you identify potential errors before your taxes are filed, and ensure that your tax preparer is claiming all allowable deductions. Softbound, 80 pgs.

#101025-CK26 $21.95

The Business of Family Child Care: Contracts and Policies
Most family child care providers would rather care for children than write and enforce contracts and policies, but taking care of the children is only part of the job. Contracts and policies are another important part of running a business. This video can help you understand how to establish a good business relationship with the families you serve by creating clear contracts and policies and enforcing them fairly.

#548029-CK26 $49.95

The Business of Family Child Care: Record-Keeping
Most family child care providers would rather care for children than spend time keeping records. But record keeping is an important part of running a business. This training video can help you understand proper record-keeping strategies, help lower taxes, and save family child care providers money.

#547329-CK26 $79.95

Family Child Care Record-Keeping Guide, 9th Edition
Keep your business organized with the latest information and advice to help you maintain important records. This edition includes descriptions of new depreciation rules, clarifications on deductions, updated resource links, and much more. Softbound, 216 pgs.

#543970-CK26 $21.95

Family Child Care Contracts and Policies, 4th Edition
This edition of the family child care classic offers expanded information on handling rates, late payments, and other fees in your contract; resolving disputes with clients; writing comprehensive policies; and enforcing and terminating your contract. Softbound, 184 pgs.

#546506-CK26 $21.95

Family Child Care Marketing Guide, 2nd Edition
Maximize your enrollment and find inexpensive ways to promote your business. Dozens of marketing tips, information on setting rates, and guidance for using electronic media are included. Softbound, 216 pgs.

#541129-CK26 $18.95

Family Child Care Legal and Insurance Guide
From purchasing insurance to incorporating your business, this indispensable guide details the ways you can reduce the risks and ensure the health and prosperity of your business. Softbound, 224 pgs.

#108501-CK26 $21.95

Family Child Care Business Planning Guide
Whether you are just starting out or have an established operation, a business plan is an essential tool for success. Find information on how to write and use your plan to effectively manage your business. Softbound, 96 pgs.

#112901-CK26 $21.95

Family Child Care Money Management and Retirement Guide
Find valuable information for your business, including how to earn more money and reduce your expenses, plan for retirement, and handle special financial situations. Softbound, 208 pgs.

#112801-CK26 $18.95

OCTOBER

Art in Our Hearts
With paint and pencil we make art—
Our work shows what's in our heart.

Recipes

Cheesy Egg, Sausage, and Potato Casserole

3 eggs
2 tablespoons low-fat milk
6 tablespoons shredded reduced-fat cheddar cheese
1 cup diced fresh red bell peppers
1⅓ cups frozen diced potatoes, thawed
½ teaspoon each onion powder and garlic powder
¾ cup mild Italian sausage, no more than 35% fat

1. Preheat oven to 375° F. Spray a loaf pan with nonstick cooking spray.
2. In a small bowl, combine eggs, milk, and cheese. Whisk to mix. Set aside.
3. In a small bowl, combine bell peppers, thawed potatoes, onion powder, and garlic powder. Mix and set aside.
4. Heat a medium skillet on medium-high heat. Add Italian sausage. Crumble with a spoon as it cooks. Cook until golden brown, about 5 minutes. Drain grease and discard.
5. Add bell pepper and potato mixture to skillet. Stir frequently. Cook for 3–5 minutes or until bell peppers begin to soften.
6. Transfer vegetable-sausage mixture to the loaf pan. Allow mixture to cool for about 5 minutes.
7. Add egg mixture. Stir to mix.
8. Bake for 20 minutes. Heat to an internal temperature of 165° F.

Yield: 6 servings
Meal Component: Meat/Meat Alternate

Quick Quesadillas

2½ cups frozen spinach (thawed and drained yields 1½ cups)
1 cup canned no-salt kidney beans, drained and rinsed
1 teaspoon garlic powder
½ teaspoon onion powder
¼ teaspoon chili powder
4 8-inch whole grain tortillas (at least 51 grams each)
1½ cups shredded low-fat mozzarella cheese

1. Preheat oven to 350° F.
2. Thaw, drain, and squeeze excess liquid from spinach, then chop.
3. Place kidney beans in a small microwavable bowl. Add garlic powder, onion powder, and chili powder. Lightly mash beans (at least 50% of the beans should appear whole). Heat in microwave for 1 minute. Stir with a spoon.
4. Prepare quesadillas: Place 2 of the tortillas on a baking sheet. Spread ¾ cup of spinach on each tortilla. Top each with ⅜ cup of bean mixture and ¾ cup of cheese. Place remaining 2 tortillas on top.
5. Spray outside of filled quesadillas with nonstick cooking spray. Bake for 15 minutes. Heat to an internal temperature of 140° F. Remove from the oven. Cut each quesadilla into 6 wedges. Serve 2 wedges or ⅓ quesadilla.

Yield: 6 servings
Meal Component: Meat/Meat Alternate, Grain, Vegetable

Nutrition and Fitness Notes

Fruits and vegetables are loaded with vitamins and minerals. Choose fruits and vegetables in a variety of colors: yellow, green, red, white, purple, orange, and more!

Serving sizes are for ages 3–5. Guidelines for the proper credit of food may vary in some states. Please check with the CACFP in your state for more information.

Menu of the Month

Breakfast
Milk
Cheesy Egg, Sausage, and Potato Casserole*
Cherry Tomatoes

Morning Snack
Water
Oatmeal (WG)
Tangerines

Lunch
Milk
Quick Quesadillas* (WG)
Honeydew Melon

Afternoon Snack
Water
Pear Slices
Whole Grain Granola (WG)

*Indicates recipes of the month.
(WG) Indicates whole grain.
Recipes adapted from the Institute of Childhood Nutrition.

The Experienced Provider

Some educators decorate the foyers of their homes with the art created by the children in their programs. Periodically mount children's art, place it in glass-covered frames, and hang it in your entryway. Not only are the pictures colorful and actually quite lovely in their frames, but the children will be proud of their artwork and how it is presented. You can change the artwork every month. The children will come to anticipate each new art show.

Activities for Children

Everyday Art
Keep simple art supplies available, such as scrap paper for drawing, old boxes to cut up for cardboard canvas, or pieces of cloth for pasted-up designs or patchwork. Let children express themselves. A picture does not have to look like something you recognize. Have them practice different techniques, including drawing with lines, shaping figures, and designing with blocks of color.

Nature Mobile
Go on a nature search and ask the children to find interesting sticks and other items such as pine cones and colorful leaves. Cut several lengths of yarn. Tie one piece of yarn to the middle of the stick for a hanger, and then tie on the other objects so they hang down from the stick to create the mobile.

Class Mural
Roll out a piece of butcher paper and place it on the carpet so each child has their own space to work. Provide each child with a large nontoxic glue stick and give them shades of brown and black paper, magazine clippings showing various skin tones, and any other art materials you see fit. Then display this artwork that celebrates dark colors and diverse skin tones.

Literacy Corner

The Noisy Paint Box by Barb Rosenstock
In this exuberant celebration of creativity, this book tells the fascinating story of Vasily Kandinsky, one of the very first painters of abstract art.

Mouse Paint by Ellen Stoll Walsh
One day three white mice discover three jars of paint—red, blue, and yellow. Both parents and children alike will appreciate this lighthearted presentation of a lesson in color.

OCTOBER ATTENDANCE AND PAYMENT LOG

To record drop-off and pickup times that vary, try using two lines per child.

CHILD'S NAME	S	M	T	W	T 1	F 2	S 3	TOTAL	S 4	M 5	T 6	W 7	T 8	F 9	S 10	TOTAL	S 11	M 12	T 13	W 14	T 15	F 16	S 17	TOTAL	S 18	M 19	T 20	W 21	T 22	F 23	S 24	TOTAL	S 25	M 26	T 27	W 28	T 29	F 30	S 31	TOTAL	S	M

OCTOBER ATTENDANCE AND PAYMENT LOG CONTINUED

CHILD'S NAME	S	M	T 1	W 2	T 3	F	S	TOTAL	S 4	M 5	T 6	W 7	T 8	F 9	S 10	TOTAL	S 11	M 12	T 13	W 14	T 15	F 16	S 17	TOTAL	S 18	M 19	T 20	W 21	T 22	F 23	S 24	TOTAL	S 25	M 26	T 27	W 28	T 29	F 30	S 31	TOTAL	S	M

WEEKLY PAYMENT TOTALS

	FOOD PROGRAM INCOME RECVD	PARENT FEE INCOME RECVD	OTHER INCOME RECVD		
OCTOBER INCOME				=	OCT TOTAL
BALANCE FORWARD				=	BALANCE FWD TOTAL
TOTAL Y-T-D INCOME				=	TOTAL Y-T-D

Food Program Claim

Date Claim Sent _____

Date Check Received _____

MEAL COUNT TALLY

BREAKFASTS	
LUNCHES	
DINNERS	
SNACKS	

Put totals in year-end meal tally, page 95.

OCTOBER EXPENSE REPORT

DATE	PAYMENT TYPE cash, check #, cc #, debit	PURCHASED FROM	PURCHASE TOTAL	ADVERTISING	INSURANCE	INTEREST	LEGAL & PROFESSIONAL SERVICES	OFFICE EXPENSES (including internet & 2nd phone)	RENT OF BUSINESS PROPERTY	REPAIR & MAINTENANCE	SUPPLIES		MILES
		THIS MONTH'S TOTAL											
		BALANCE CARRIED FORWARD											
		YEAR-TO-DATE TOTAL											

OCTOBER EXPENSE REPORT

DATE	PAYMENT TYPE cash, check #, cc #, debit	PURCHASED FROM	PURCHASE TOTAL	TAXES & LICENSES	TRAVEL & ENTERTAINMENT	FOOD	TOYS	HOUSEHOLD ITEMS	CLEANING SUPPLIES	ACTIVITY EXPENSES			MILES
		THIS MONTH'S TOTAL											
		BALANCE CARRIED FORWARD											
		YEAR-TO-DATE TOTAL											

See page 85 for an explanation of how to transfer expenses to your tax forms.
You may wish to relabel the columns to fit your business needs.

See page 6 for an explanation of the order in which we present the categories.

NOVEMBER 2026

Hours Worked	
Previous Total	
No. Hours Open*	
Other Hours Worked**	
Year-to-Date Total	

* "No. Hours Open" refers to hours from when the first child arrived to when the last child left (not your advertised work hours).
** "Other Hours Worked" refers to hours spent on business activities in the home (cleaning, meal preparation, activity planning, and so on) when children are not present.

SUN	MON	TUE	WED	THU	FRI	SAT
1 American Indian Heritage Month; All Saints' Day (Catholic); Día de los Muertos	**2** All Souls' Day (Catholic); Fire Drill Day	**3** Election Day	**4**	**5**	**6**	**7**
8 Diwalli (Hindu)	**9**	**10**	**11** Veterans Day; Severe Storm Drill Day	**12**	**13**	**14**
15	**16**	**17**	**18**	**19**	**20** Universal Children's Day	**21**
22	**23**	**24**	**25**	**26** Thanksgiving Day	**27**	**28**
29 First Sunday of Advent (Christian)	**30** Call your local R & R agency; update your service					

Be ready for 2027. Order your *Redleaf Calendar-Keeper*™ 2027 today.

NOVEMBER

All About Babies
Watch us grow when we are small—
Roll over, sit up, creep, then crawl!

Recipes

Local Harvest Bake

2 cups peeled and cubed fresh butternut squash
2 cups peeled and cubed fresh beets
2 cups peeled and cubed fresh sweet potatoes
1 tablespoon olive oil
¾ teaspoon minced fresh garlic
½ teaspoon dried parsley (optional)

1. Preheat oven to 325° F. Line a 9-by-13-inch baking pan with parchment paper. Spray lightly with cooking spray.
2. Toss butternut squash, beets, sweet potatoes, olive oil, salt, and garlic in a medium mixing bowl. Add vegetables to prepared pan and spread evenly.
3. Bake for 25 minutes. Remove from oven. Garnish with parsley.

Yield: 6 servings, ½ cup each
Meal Component: Vegetable

Strawberry Smoothie Bowl

3 cups low-fat Greek yogurt
6 cups frozen strawberries
¼ cup agave syrup
1½ teaspoon vanilla extract

1. Pour strawberries into a high-speed blender. Puree strawberries on medium speed until strawberries have a smooth consistency.
2. Place yogurt in a large mixing bowl. Pour strawberry puree over yogurt. Stir well.
3. Add agave syrup and vanilla extract. Stir well.

Yield: 6 servings, ¾ cup each
Meal Component: Meat/Meat Alternate, Fruit

Serving sizes are for ages 3–5. Guidelines for the proper credit of food may vary in some states. Please check with the CACFP in your state for more information.

Menu of the Month

Breakfast
Milk
Whole Wheat Bagel (WG)
Canned Mixed Fruit

Morning Snack
Deli Turkey
Jicama Slices

Lunch
Milk
Local Harvest Bake*
Sloppy Joes on Whole Grain Buns (WG)
Grapes

Afternoon Snack
Strawberry Smoothie Bowls*

*Indicates recipes of the month.
(WG) Indicates whole grain.
Recipes adapted from the Institute of Childhood Nutrition.

Nutrition and Fitness Notes

When infants are hungry, they cry. Being fed and having their hunger alleviated are usually the results of their crying. Further, infants learn they not only receive food and feel better when they cry, but they also receive comfort and security as they are held and cuddled. As children grow, they can learn to recognize specific needs, such as being hungry and needing food. They can also recognize feelings, such as being sad and needing a hug. To help children make the connection between hunger and food, promote the idea that food is for hunger rather than reward or comfort.

The Experienced Provider

Infants' play should be full of exploration and discovery. Infants should be encouraged to use all their senses to examine the color, shape, texture, and movement of objects. They need the opportunity to shake things for sound, push things for movement, and place safe objects in their mouths for taste and touch. You should choose toys that stimulate their senses and allow for active involvement.

Activities for Children

Sensory Bottles
A great way to reuse plastic bottles and jars is to fill them with different fun substances or objects, such as water, glitter, and food coloring; colored water and cut straws; hair gel with braid beads; or assorted pebbles or other natural objects. Make sure the lids are tightly secured. Encourage the infants to hold, touch, lift, turn, and shake the containers. Show them how to roll the containers on a flat surface. Watch to see if they transfer the containers from one hand to another. If needed, encourage this by handing a second container to an infant—often an infant will transfer the held object to the empty hand before taking the second object.

Rattles and Sound
Experiment with lots of different sounds. Always begin by talking with the infants, saying their names and repeatedly identifying yourself. Wait for them to look in one direction. Gently shake a rattle or another safe object from the opposite direction. Note whether they turn toward the sound. Show them the object you are shaking. Tell them what the object is and help them to hold it. Then help them shake the object again.

Skin Tones in the Mirror
Affixing color swatches that closely resemble human skin colors to mirrors can encourage children to explore color diversity as they are looking at themselves. Affirm skin tones through mirror play by taping butcher paper to parts of the mirrors and giving the babies edible natural paint so that they can explore with nature colors while also looking at themselves in the mirror.

Literacy Corner

Sweetest Kulu by Celina Kalluk
Lyrically and tenderly told by a mother speaking to her own little Kulu, this visually stunning book is infused with the traditional Inuit values of love and respect for the land and its animal inhabitants.

Whose Toes Are Those? by Jabari Asim
Snuggle with a child on your lap with this cheerful rhyme inspired by the classic giggle-inspiring game of This Little Piggy.

NOVEMBER ATTENDANCE AND PAYMENT LOG

To record drop-off and pickup times that vary, try using two lines per child.

CHILD'S NAME	S 1	M 2	T 3	W 4	T 5	F 6	S 7	TOTAL	S 8	M 9	T 10	W 11	T 12	F 13	S 14	TOTAL	S 15	M 16	T 17	W 18	T 19	F 20	S 21	TOTAL	S 22	M 23	T 24	W 25	T 26	F 27	S 28	TOTAL	S 29	M 30	T	W	T	F	S	TOTAL	S	M

NOVEMBER ATTENDANCE AND PAYMENT LOG CONTINUED

CHILD'S NAME	S 1	M 2	T 3	W 4	T 5	F 6	S 7	TOTAL	S 8	M 9	T 10	W 11	T 12	F 13	S 14	TOTAL	S 15	M 16	T 17	W 18	T 19	F 20	S 21	TOTAL	S 22	M 23	T 24	W 25	T 26	F 27	S 28	TOTAL	S 29	M 30	T	W	T	F	S	TOTAL	S	M

WEEKLY PAYMENT TOTALS

	FOOD PROGRAM INCOME RECVD	PARENT FEE INCOME RECVD	OTHER INCOME RECVD			
NOVEMBER INCOME				=	NOV TOTAL	
BALANCE FORWARD				=	BALANCE FWD TOTAL	
TOTAL Y-T-D INCOME				=	TOTAL Y-T-D	

Food Program Claim

Date Claim Sent _____

Date Check Received _____

MEAL COUNT TALLY	
BREAKFASTS	
LUNCHES	
DINNERS	
SNACKS	

Put totals in year-end meal tally, page 95.

NOVEMBER EXPENSE REPORT

DATE	PAYMENT TYPE cash, check #, cc #, debit	PURCHASED FROM	PURCHASE TOTAL	ADVERTISING	INSURANCE	INTEREST	LEGAL & PROFESSIONAL SERVICES	OFFICE EXPENSES (including internet & 2nd phone)	RENT OF BUSINESS PROPERTY	REPAIR & MAINTENANCE	SUPPLIES		MILES
		THIS MONTH'S TOTAL											
		BALANCE CARRIED FORWARD											
		YEAR-TO-DATE TOTAL											

NOVEMBER EXPENSE REPORT

DATE	PAYMENT TYPE cash, check #, cc #, debit	PURCHASED FROM	PURCHASE TOTAL	TAXES & LICENSES	TRAVEL & ENTERTAINMENT	FOOD	TOYS	HOUSEHOLD ITEMS	CLEANING SUPPLIES	ACTIVITY EXPENSES			MILES
		THIS MONTH'S TOTAL											
		BALANCE CARRIED FORWARD											
		YEAR-TO-DATE TOTAL											

See page 85 for an explanation of how to transfer expenses to your tax forms.
You may wish to relabel the columns to fit your business needs.

See page 6 for an explanation of the order in which we present the categories.

DECEMBER 2026

Hours Worked	
Previous Total	
No. Hours Open*	
Other Hours Worked**	
Year-to-Date Total	

* "No. Hours Open" refers to hours from when the first child arrived to when the last child left (not your advertised work hours).
** "Other Hours Worked" refers to hours spent on business activities in the home (cleaning, meal preparation, activity planning, and so on) when children are not present.

SUN	MON	TUE	WED	THU	FRI	SAT
	Tax season is just around the corner. Don't forget to order your 2026 tax resources!	**1**	**2**	**3**	**4**	**5** Hanukkah begins (Jewish)
6	**7** Fire Drill Day	**8**	**9** Severe Storm Drill Day	**10** Human Rights Day	**11**	**12** Hanukkah ends (Jewish)
13	**14**	**15**	**16**	**17**	**18**	**19**
20	**21** Winter begins	**22**	**23**	**24** Christmas Eve (Christian)	**25** Christmas Day (Christian)	**26** Boxing Day Kwanzaa begins
27	**28**	**29**	**30** Call your local R & R agency; update your service	**31** New Year's Eve		

NOVEMBER 2026

S	M	T	W	T	F	S
1	2	3	4	5	6	7
8	9	10	11	12	13	14
15	16	17	18	19	20	21
22	23	24	25	26	27	28
29	30					

JANUARY 2027

S	M	T	W	T	F	S
					1	2
3	4	5	6	7	8	9
10	11	12	13	14	15	16
17	18	19	20	21	22	23
24	25	26	27	28	29	30
31						

DECEMBER

Sensory Play

With sensory play we learn so much,
Through sight and sound, smell, taste, and touch

Recipes

Lemon-Blueberry Muffins

⅔ cup whole wheat flour
¼ cup enriched cornmeal
¼ cup brown sugar
¼ teaspoon salt
1 teaspoon baking powder
½ cup low-fat milk
¼ cup unsweetened applesauce
1 egg
¼ teaspoon lemon extract
½ cup blueberries (fresh or frozen)

1. Preheat oven to 375° F. Line muffin tins with paper liners. Spray with nonstick cooking spray.
2. In a medium bowl, combine flour, cornmeal, brown sugar, salt, and baking powder. Sift mixture. Remove 1 tablespoon of dry mixture and set aside.
3. In a small bowl, combine milk, applesauce, egg, and lemon extract. Whisk until well blended. Add to dry ingredients. Whisk to mix.
4. Place frozen blueberries in a small bowl. Add reserved dry mixture and toss.
5. With a rubber spatula, fold breaded blueberries and any remaining dry ingredients from the bottom of the bowl into the muffin mixture. Pour ⅓ cup of muffin mixture into each prepared muffin liner.
6. Bake for 25 minutes. Remove from the oven and cool on a rack for 5 minutes.

Yield: 6 servings, 1 muffin each
Meal Component: Grain

Baked Carrot Fries with Yogurt Dip

4 cups fresh baby carrots
1½ teaspoon canola oil
¾ cup plus 1 tablespoon nonfat plain Greek yogurt
3 tablespoons sunflower seed butter

1. Preheat oven to 400° F.
2. In a small bowl, combine carrots and oil with salt to taste. Toss.
3. Place carrots on a baking sheet in a single layer. Bake for 20 minutes or until lightly brown on the bottom.
4. In a small bowl, combine yogurt and sunflower seed butter. Use a fork or rubber spatula to mix until smooth.
5. Serve ½ cup carrot fries (about 6–10) and 2 tablespoons dip.

Yield: 6 servings, ½ cup each
Meal Component: Meat/Meat Alternate, Vegetable

Nutrition and Fitness Notes

Children explore food with all their senses. First, they see and smell the food. Fresh produce provides a rainbow of colors. The smell of a grilling hamburger or baking cookies may entice children to run and see what is cooking. Children then hear the sounds produced by the food, such as crackers breaking, fish sizzling, and apples crunching. Next, they explore the food's texture and temperature, first with their fingers and then with their lips and tongues. Finally, children taste the food and discover whether it is sweet, sour, salty, or spicy.

Menu of the Month

Breakfast
Milk
Lemon-Blueberry Muffins* (WG)
Clementines

Morning Snack
Water
Baked Carrot Fries with Yogurt Dip*

Lunch
Milk
Chicken Tacos in Whole Grain Tortillas (WG)
Avocado Slices
Pineapple

Afternoon Snack
Water
Whole Grain-Rich Puffed Cereal
Apple Chunks with Pomegranate Seeds

*Indicates recipes of the month.
(WG) Indicates whole grain.
Recipes adapted from the Institute of Childhood Nutrition.

Serving sizes are for ages 3–5. Guidelines for the proper credit of food may vary in some states. Please check with the CACFP in your state for more information.

The Experienced Provider

Providing a selection of open-ended materials (also called *loose parts*) is budget friendly and helps save you from amassing large quantities of single-purpose stuff you only occasionally use. Open-ended materials also give children free rein to show their creativity and imagination. Play around with your ratios of open-ended to representational materials until you find the mix that works best for you, your space, and the children in your care.

Activities for Children

Weather and Our Senses

Talk about the weather. What is weather? Weather is the condition of the air in a particular place at a specific time. To young children, weather is what they see, hear, and feel when they are outside. Talk about seasons and what the weather is like each day. Encourage children to talk about how it feels to be cold or hot. Ask children to explain what they see and feel as seasons change.

Busy Boxes

Infants need play materials that stimulate their senses. Make busy boxes filled with safe, infant-friendly materials and place them in learning centers. Include brightly colored fine-motor toys (balls, stacking/nesting cups), mirrors, or levers to manipulate. A busy box should not be a substitute for caregiver interaction.

Hair Texture Play

Fill empty tissue boxes with interesting items for toddlers to feel. Select items related to different hair textures, such as cotton for Afro hair; braided yarn for braids, twists, or locs; curled ribbon for curly hair; and strips of paper for straight hair. Or turn it into a matching game: toddlers are given pictures of Afro, braided, curly, and straight hair and encouraged to match the pictures to the box with items that feel similar to each hair type.

Literacy Corner

Quiet! by Kate Alizadeh
The text and sensory clues in this picture book allow children to experience their home through the many noises it makes.

Baby Loves the Five Senses: Sight! by Ruth Spiro
Accurate enough for experts, yet simple enough for baby, this clever board book explores the science of vision, light, and color.

DECEMBER ATTENDANCE AND PAYMENT LOG

To record drop-off and pickup times that vary, try using two lines per child.

CHILD'S NAME	S	M	T 1	W 2	T 3	F 4	S 5	TOTAL	S 6	M 7	T 8	W 9	T 10	F 11	S 12	TOTAL	S 13	M 14	T 15	W 16	T 17	F 18	S 19	TOTAL	S 20	M 21	T 22	W 23	T 24	F 25	S 26	TOTAL	S 27	M 28	T 29	W 30	T 31	F	S	TOTAL	S	M		

DECEMBER ATTENDANCE AND PAYMENT LOG CONTINUED

CHILD'S NAME	S	M	T 1	W 2	T 3	F 4	S 5	TOTAL	S 6	M 7	T 8	W 9	T 10	F 11	S 12	TOTAL	S 13	M 14	T 15	W 16	T 17	F 18	S 19	TOTAL	S 20	M 21	T 22	W 23	T 24	F 25	S 26	TOTAL	S 27	M 28	T 29	W 30	T 31	F	S	TOTAL	S	M

WEEKLY PAYMENT TOTALS

	FOOD PROGRAM INCOME RECVD	PARENT FEE INCOME RECVD	OTHER INCOME RECVD			
DECEMBER INCOME				=	DEC TOTAL	
BALANCE FORWARD				=	BALANCE FWD TOTAL	
TOTAL Y-T-D INCOME				=	TOTAL Y-T-D	

Food Program Claim

Date Claim Sent _____

Date Check Received _____

MEAL COUNT TALLY	
BREAKFASTS	
LUNCHES	
DINNERS	
SNACKS	

Put totals in year-end meal tally, page 95.

DECEMBER EXPENSE REPORT

DATE	PAYMENT TYPE cash, check #, cc #, debit	PURCHASED FROM	PURCHASE TOTAL	ADVERTISING	INSURANCE	INTEREST	LEGAL & PROFESSIONAL SERVICES	OFFICE EXPENSES (including internet & 2nd phone)	RENT OF BUSINESS PROPERTY	REPAIR & MAINTENANCE	SUPPLIES		MILES
		THIS MONTH'S TOTAL											
		BALANCE CARRIED FORWARD											
		YEAR-TO-DATE TOTAL											

DECEMBER EXPENSE REPORT

DATE	PAYMENT TYPE cash, check #, cc #, debit	PURCHASED FROM	PURCHASE TOTAL	TAXES & LICENSES	TRAVEL & ENTERTAINMENT	FOOD	TOYS	HOUSEHOLD ITEMS	CLEANING SUPPLIES	ACTIVITY EXPENSES			MILES
		THIS MONTH'S TOTAL											
		BALANCE CARRIED FORWARD											
		YEAR-TO-DATE TOTAL											

See page 85 for an explanation of how to transfer expenses to your tax forms. You may wish to relabel the columns to fit your business needs.

See page 6 for an explanation of the order in which we present the categories.

HOUSE EXPENSES WORKSHEET

YEAR:	Natural Gas		Electricity		Water/Sewer		Trash Collection		Cable TV	
	Date Paid	Amount	Date Paid	Amount	Date Paid	Amount	Date Paid	Amount	Date Paid	Amount
JANUARY										
FEBRUARY										
MARCH										
APRIL										
MAY										
JUNE										
JULY										
AUGUST										
SEPTEMBER										
OCTOBER										
NOVEMBER										
DECEMBER										
TOTAL										
TIME-SPACE PERCENTAGE										
FCC BUSINESS EXPENSE										

Homeowners Insurance		Property Taxes		Mortgage Interest or Rent		House Repairs & Maintenance	
Date Paid	Amount	Date Paid	Amount	Date Paid	Amount	Date Paid	Amount

NOTE: You are entitled to claim a portion of these house expenses for your business. Use this worksheet to record these expenses each month or once a year. For each column, fill in the total and your Time-Space percentage (to compute, see the *Family Child Care Record-Keeping Guide*, 9th edition). To arrive at the FCC business expense, multiply the total in each column by the Time-Space percentage.

Add together the FCC business expenses for natural gas, electricity, water/sewer, trash collection, and cable TV, and enter the total under Utilities on the next page. Take the totals of the other FCC business expense columns and enter them on the next page. When you file your taxes, the house expenses on this page go directly onto Form 8829 Expenses for Business Use of Your Home.

INCOME TAX WORKSHEET

TOTAL INCOME (See December Year-to-Date Total. Enter directly onto Form 1040 Schedule C.)	
EXPENSES	
I. DIRECT BUSINESS EXPENSES (See monthly expense reports. Enter directly onto Form 1040 Schedule C.)	
ADVERTISING	
CAR AND TRUCK EXPENSES (Include mileage and the business portion of any car-loan interest or excise tax.)	
LIABILITY INSURANCE	
BUSINESS INTEREST (not mortgage interest) (credit card interest on business portion of purchases)	
LEGAL AND PROFESSIONAL SERVICES	
OFFICE EXPENSES (postage, bank charges, education and training, dues, publications)	
RENT OF BUSINESS PROPERTY (other than home or apartment) (videos, carpet shampooer)	
REPAIRS AND MAINTENANCE OF PERSONAL PROPERTY (furniture, appliances, equipment)	
SUPPLIES	
TAXES AND LICENSES	
TRAVEL AND ENTERTAINMENT (for overnight conferences)	
FOOD (List under Other Expenses on Form 1040 Schedule C.)	
TOYS (List under Other Expenses on Form 1040 Schedule C.)	
HOUSEHOLD ITEMS, CLEANING SUPPLIES, AND ACTIVITY EXPENSES (List under Other Expenses on Form 1040 Schedule C.)	
II. HOUSE EXPENSES (See page 84. Enter directly onto Form 8829.)	
UTILITIES	
HOMEOWNERS INSURANCE	
PROPERTY TAXES	
MORTGAGE INTEREST OR RENT	
HOUSE REPAIRS AND MAINTENANCE (painting, broken glass)	
III. DEPRECIATION EXPENSES (Enter directly onto Form 8829 or Form 4562.)	
HOUSE (Form 8829)	
HOME IMPROVEMENTS (Form 4562) (new roof, furnace, remodeling)	
LAND IMPROVEMENTS (Form 4562 or Schedule C) (fence, driveway)	
TOTAL EXPENSES (deductions)	
NET INCOME (income minus expenses)	

How to Use This Worksheet

Use this worksheet at the end of the year to pull together all of your business expenses recorded on this *Redleaf Calendar-Keeper*. The categories of expenses listed here correspond to particular lines on the various tax forms that you must fill out for your business. Enter direct business expenses on Form 1040 Schedule C. Enter house expenses on Form 8829. Enter depreciation expenses on Form 8829 or Form 4562. After you have completed Forms 8829 and 4562, you will enter the totals from these forms onto your Schedule C.

You may wish to add or move some direct business expenses to different categories than are shown on this worksheet. Sometimes you may have two or more different expense categories on one receipt. You may either split the receipt and list items under more than one category or list all the expenses under one category. It doesn't matter which method you choose because all direct business expenses get totaled at the bottom of the Schedule C. You will not be penalized by the IRS for listing a supply expense under the food category or vice versa.

There are special rules concerning depreciation expenses. For a description of how to calculate depreciation expenses, see the *Family Child Care 2026 Tax Workbook and Organizer*.

PAYMENT AND INCOME RECORD FOR JANUARY–MARCH

CHILD'S NAME	JANUARY					JAN TOTAL	FEBRUARY					FEB TOTAL	MARCH					MAR TOTAL	1st Qtr* Total
SUBTOTALS																			
FOOD PROGRAM																			
OTHER INCOME																			
TOTALS																			

*1st quarter for estimated tax for the months of January–March. For income tax purposes, quarters are determined by the federal government and are not always the same as calendar quarters. Taxes for the 1st quarter are due April 15.

If you receive payments from a third party (such as a government agency) and don't get paid until a later month, use two lines per child and enter the payment date and check number on the second line.

PAYMENT AND INCOME RECORD FOR JANUARY–MARCH CONTINUED

CHILD'S NAME	JANUARY						JAN TOTAL	FEBRUARY						FEB TOTAL	MARCH						MAR TOTAL	1st Qtr* Total
SUBTOTALS																						
FOOD PROGRAM																						
OTHER INCOME																						
TOTALS																						

*1st quarter for estimated tax for the months of January–March. For income tax purposes, quarters are determined by the federal government and are not always the same as calendar quarters. Taxes for the 1st quarter are due April 15.

PAYMENT AND INCOME RECORD FOR APRIL–JUNE

CHILD'S NAME	APRIL						APR TOTAL	MAY						MAY TOTAL	2nd Qtr* TOTAL	JUNE						JUN TOTAL
SUBTOTALS																						
FOOD PROGRAM																						
OTHER INCOME																						
TOTALS																						

*2nd quarter for estimated tax for the months of April and May. For income tax purposes, quarters are determined by the federal government and are not always the same as calendar quarters. Taxes for the 2nd quarter are due June 15.

BALANCE CARRIED FORWARD

YEAR-TO-DATE TOTAL

PAYMENT AND INCOME RECORD FOR APRIL–JUNE CONTINUED

CHILD'S NAME	APRIL						APR TOTAL	MAY						MAY TOTAL	2nd Qtr* TOTAL	JUNE						JUN TOTAL
SUBTOTALS																						
FOOD PROGRAM																						
OTHER INCOME																						
TOTALS																						

*2nd quarter for estimated tax for the months of April and May. For income tax purposes, quarters are determined by the federal government and are not always the same as calendar quarters. Taxes for the 2nd quarter are due June 15.

BALANCE CARRIED FORWARD

YEAR-TO-DATE TOTAL

PAYMENT AND INCOME RECORD FOR JULY–SEPTEMBER

CHILD'S NAME	JULY						JUL TOTAL	AUGUST						AUG TOTAL	3rd Qtr* TOTAL	SEPTEMBER						SEP TOTAL
SUBTOTALS																						
FOOD PROGRAM																						
OTHER INCOME																						
TOTALS																						

*3rd quarter for estimated tax for the months of June–August. For income tax purposes, quarters are determined by the federal government and are not always the same as calendar quarters. Taxes for the 3rd quarter are due September 15.

BALANCE CARRIED FORWARD

YEAR-TO-DATE TOTAL

PAYMENT AND INCOME RECORD FOR JULY–SEPTEMBER CONTINUED

CHILD'S NAME	JULY						JUL TOTAL	AUGUST						AUG TOTAL	3rd Qtr* TOTAL	SEPTEMBER						SEP TOTAL
SUBTOTALS																						
FOOD PROGRAM																						
OTHER INCOME																						
TOTALS																						

BALANCE CARRIED FORWARD

YEAR-TO-DATE TOTAL

*3rd quarter for estimated tax for the months of June–August. For income tax purposes, quarters are determined by the federal government and are not always the same as calendar quarters. Taxes for the 3rd quarter are due September 15.

PAYMENT AND INCOME RECORD FOR OCTOBER–DECEMBER

CHILD'S NAME	OCTOBER						OCT TOTAL	NOVEMBER						NOV TOTAL	DECEMBER						DEC TOTAL	4th Qtr* TOTAL
SUBTOTALS																						
FOOD PROGRAM																						
OTHER INCOME																						
TOTALS																						

*4th quarter for estimated tax for the months of September–December. For income tax purposes, quarters are determined by the federal government and are not always the same as calendar quarters. Taxes for the 4th quarter are due January 15, 2027.

Income should be reported as income in the year you receive it, not the year you earn it. Payments received after December 31, 2025, for child care services you delivered in 2025 should be reported as income in 2026.

BALANCE CARRIED FORWARD

2026 TOTAL

PAYMENT AND INCOME RECORD FOR OCTOBER–DECEMBER CONTINUED

CHILD'S NAME	OCTOBER						OCT TOTAL	NOVEMBER						NOV TOTAL	DECEMBER						DEC TOTAL	4th Qtr* TOTAL
SUBTOTALS																						
FOOD PROGRAM																						
OTHER INCOME																						
TOTALS																						

*4th quarter for estimated tax for the months of September–December. For income tax purposes, quarters are determined by the federal government and are not always the same as calendar quarters. Taxes for the 4th quarter are due January 15, 2027.

Income should be reported as income in the year you receive it, not the year you earn it. Payments received after December 31, 2025, for child care services you delivered in 2025 should be reported as income in 2026.

BALANCE CARRIED FORWARD

2026 TOTAL

MEAL FORM Week of _____ 2026

Child	Mon	Tue	Wed	Thu	Fri	Sat	Sun	Totals	Child	Mon	Tue	Wed	Thu	Fri	Sat	Sun	Totals
	Bkst ___ Lun ___ Din ___ Sn1 ___ Sn2 ___ Sn3 ___	Bkst ___ Lun ___ Din ___ Sn1 ___ Sn2 ___ Sn3 ___	Bkst ___ Lun ___ Din ___ Sn1 ___ Sn2 ___ Sn3 ___	Bkst ___ Lun ___ Din ___ Sn1 ___ Sn2 ___ Sn3 ___	Bkst ___ Lun ___ Din ___ Sn1 ___ Sn2 ___ Sn3 ___	Bkst ___ Lun ___ Din ___ Sn1 ___ Sn2 ___ Sn3 ___	Bkst ___ Lun ___ Din ___ Sn1 ___ Sn2 ___ Sn3 ___	B ___ L ___ D ___ S ___		Bkst ___ Lun ___ Din ___ Sn1 ___ Sn2 ___ Sn3 ___	Bkst ___ Lun ___ Din ___ Sn1 ___ Sn2 ___ Sn3 ___	Bkst ___ Lun ___ Din ___ Sn1 ___ Sn2 ___ Sn3 ___	Bkst ___ Lun ___ Din ___ Sn1 ___ Sn2 ___ Sn3 ___	Bkst ___ Lun ___ Din ___ Sn1 ___ Sn2 ___ Sn3 ___	Bkst ___ Lun ___ Din ___ Sn1 ___ Sn2 ___ Sn3 ___	Bkst ___ Lun ___ Din ___ Sn1 ___ Sn2 ___ Sn3 ___	B ___ L ___ D ___ S ___
	Bkst ___ Lun ___ Din ___ Sn1 ___ Sn2 ___ Sn3 ___	Bkst ___ Lun ___ Din ___ Sn1 ___ Sn2 ___ Sn3 ___	Bkst ___ Lun ___ Din ___ Sn1 ___ Sn2 ___ Sn3 ___	Bkst ___ Lun ___ Din ___ Sn1 ___ Sn2 ___ Sn3 ___	Bkst ___ Lun ___ Din ___ Sn1 ___ Sn2 ___ Sn3 ___	Bkst ___ Lun ___ Din ___ Sn1 ___ Sn2 ___ Sn3 ___	Bkst ___ Lun ___ Din ___ Sn1 ___ Sn2 ___ Sn3 ___	B ___ L ___ D ___ S ___		Bkst ___ Lun ___ Din ___ Sn1 ___ Sn2 ___ Sn3 ___	Bkst ___ Lun ___ Din ___ Sn1 ___ Sn2 ___ Sn3 ___	Bkst ___ Lun ___ Din ___ Sn1 ___ Sn2 ___ Sn3 ___	Bkst ___ Lun ___ Din ___ Sn1 ___ Sn2 ___ Sn3 ___	Bkst ___ Lun ___ Din ___ Sn1 ___ Sn2 ___ Sn3 ___	Bkst ___ Lun ___ Din ___ Sn1 ___ Sn2 ___ Sn3 ___	Bkst ___ Lun ___ Din ___ Sn1 ___ Sn2 ___ Sn3 ___	B ___ L ___ D ___ S ___
	Bkst ___ Lun ___ Din ___ Sn1 ___ Sn2 ___ Sn3 ___	Bkst ___ Lun ___ Din ___ Sn1 ___ Sn2 ___ Sn3 ___	Bkst ___ Lun ___ Din ___ Sn1 ___ Sn2 ___ Sn3 ___	Bkst ___ Lun ___ Din ___ Sn1 ___ Sn2 ___ Sn3 ___	Bkst ___ Lun ___ Din ___ Sn1 ___ Sn2 ___ Sn3 ___	Bkst ___ Lun ___ Din ___ Sn1 ___ Sn2 ___ Sn3 ___	Bkst ___ Lun ___ Din ___ Sn1 ___ Sn2 ___ Sn3 ___	B ___ L ___ D ___ S ___		Bkst ___ Lun ___ Din ___ Sn1 ___ Sn2 ___ Sn3 ___	Bkst ___ Lun ___ Din ___ Sn1 ___ Sn2 ___ Sn3 ___	Bkst ___ Lun ___ Din ___ Sn1 ___ Sn2 ___ Sn3 ___	Bkst ___ Lun ___ Din ___ Sn1 ___ Sn2 ___ Sn3 ___	Bkst ___ Lun ___ Din ___ Sn1 ___ Sn2 ___ Sn3 ___	Bkst ___ Lun ___ Din ___ Sn1 ___ Sn2 ___ Sn3 ___	Bkst ___ Lun ___ Din ___ Sn1 ___ Sn2 ___ Sn3 ___	B ___ L ___ D ___ S ___
	Bkst ___ Lun ___ Din ___ Sn1 ___ Sn2 ___ Sn3 ___	Bkst ___ Lun ___ Din ___ Sn1 ___ Sn2 ___ Sn3 ___	Bkst ___ Lun ___ Din ___ Sn1 ___ Sn2 ___ Sn3 ___	Bkst ___ Lun ___ Din ___ Sn1 ___ Sn2 ___ Sn3 ___	Bkst ___ Lun ___ Din ___ Sn1 ___ Sn2 ___ Sn3 ___	Bkst ___ Lun ___ Din ___ Sn1 ___ Sn2 ___ Sn3 ___	Bkst ___ Lun ___ Din ___ Sn1 ___ Sn2 ___ Sn3 ___	B ___ L ___ D ___ S ___		Bkst ___ Lun ___ Din ___ Sn1 ___ Sn2 ___ Sn3 ___	Bkst ___ Lun ___ Din ___ Sn1 ___ Sn2 ___ Sn3 ___	Bkst ___ Lun ___ Din ___ Sn1 ___ Sn2 ___ Sn3 ___	Bkst ___ Lun ___ Din ___ Sn1 ___ Sn2 ___ Sn3 ___	Bkst ___ Lun ___ Din ___ Sn1 ___ Sn2 ___ Sn3 ___	Bkst ___ Lun ___ Din ___ Sn1 ___ Sn2 ___ Sn3 ___	Bkst ___ Lun ___ Din ___ Sn1 ___ Sn2 ___ Sn3 ___	B ___ L ___ D ___ S ___
	Bkst ___ Lun ___ Din ___ Sn1 ___ Sn2 ___ Sn3 ___	Bkst ___ Lun ___ Din ___ Sn1 ___ Sn2 ___ Sn3 ___	Bkst ___ Lun ___ Din ___ Sn1 ___ Sn2 ___ Sn3 ___	Bkst ___ Lun ___ Din ___ Sn1 ___ Sn2 ___ Sn3 ___	Bkst ___ Lun ___ Din ___ Sn1 ___ Sn2 ___ Sn3 ___	Bkst ___ Lun ___ Din ___ Sn1 ___ Sn2 ___ Sn3 ___	Bkst ___ Lun ___ Din ___ Sn1 ___ Sn2 ___ Sn3 ___	B ___ L ___ D ___ S ___		Bkst ___ Lun ___ Din ___ Sn1 ___ Sn2 ___ Sn3 ___	Bkst ___ Lun ___ Din ___ Sn1 ___ Sn2 ___ Sn3 ___	Bkst ___ Lun ___ Din ___ Sn1 ___ Sn2 ___ Sn3 ___	Bkst ___ Lun ___ Din ___ Sn1 ___ Sn2 ___ Sn3 ___	Bkst ___ Lun ___ Din ___ Sn1 ___ Sn2 ___ Sn3 ___	Bkst ___ Lun ___ Din ___ Sn1 ___ Sn2 ___ Sn3 ___	Bkst ___ Lun ___ Din ___ Sn1 ___ Sn2 ___ Sn3 ___	B ___ L ___ D ___ S ___
	Bkst ___ Lun ___ Din ___ Sn1 ___ Sn2 ___ Sn3 ___	Bkst ___ Lun ___ Din ___ Sn1 ___ Sn2 ___ Sn3 ___	Bkst ___ Lun ___ Din ___ Sn1 ___ Sn2 ___ Sn3 ___	Bkst ___ Lun ___ Din ___ Sn1 ___ Sn2 ___ Sn3 ___	Bkst ___ Lun ___ Din ___ Sn1 ___ Sn2 ___ Sn3 ___	Bkst ___ Lun ___ Din ___ Sn1 ___ Sn2 ___ Sn3 ___	Bkst ___ Lun ___ Din ___ Sn1 ___ Sn2 ___ Sn3 ___	B ___ L ___ D ___ S ___		Bkst ___ Lun ___ Din ___ Sn1 ___ Sn2 ___ Sn3 ___	Bkst ___ Lun ___ Din ___ Sn1 ___ Sn2 ___ Sn3 ___	Bkst ___ Lun ___ Din ___ Sn1 ___ Sn2 ___ Sn3 ___	Bkst ___ Lun ___ Din ___ Sn1 ___ Sn2 ___ Sn3 ___	Bkst ___ Lun ___ Din ___ Sn1 ___ Sn2 ___ Sn3 ___	Bkst ___ Lun ___ Din ___ Sn1 ___ Sn2 ___ Sn3 ___	Bkst ___ Lun ___ Din ___ Sn1 ___ Sn2 ___ Sn3 ___	B ___ L ___ D ___ S ___

Place a check mark (✓) next to each meal or snack you serve. Do not count meals served to your own children. If you are on the Food Program, use this form to track your nonreimbursed meals only. Add the reimbursed meals from your monthly claim forms and the nonreimbursed meals from this form together, and put the totals on the year-end meal tally on page 95. If you are not on the Food Program, use this form to track all your meals, and put the totals on the year-end meal tally on page 95.

Make copies of this form for each week of the year. If you have six or fewer children in your program, you can use one form for two weeks. You can download this form at the Redleaf Press website. Go to www.redleafpress.org, and find the page for the *Redleaf Calendar-Keeper 2026*. There will be a link to this form.

Weekly Totals

Breakfasts _____   Dinners _____

Lunches _____   Snacks _____

YEAR-END MEAL TALLY

If you are not on the Food Program, enter all meals and snacks in the column labeled "Number Not Reimbursed by Food Program."

	Breakfasts		Lunches		Dinners		Snacks	
	Number Reimbursed by Food Program	Number Not Reimbursed by Food Program	Number Reimbursed by Food Program	Number Not Reimbursed by Food Program	Number Reimbursed by Food Program	Number Not Reimbursed by Food Program	Number Reimbursed by Food Program	Number Not Reimbursed by Food Program
January								
February								
March								
April								
May								
June								
July								
August								
September								
October								
November								
December								
TOTAL								

2026 Standard Meal Allowance Rate*

Number of Breakfasts _____ X $1.70 = $_____
Number of Lunches _____ X $3.22 = $_____
Number of Dinners _____ X $3.22 = $_____
Number of Snacks _____ X $0.96 = $_____
Total Food Deductions $_____ †

Do not report any meals served to your own children (even if they are reimbursed by the Food Program).

* The IRS standard meal allowance rate for 2026 used in these calculations is based on the Tier I rate as of January 1, 2026. This rate is used for all meals and snacks served throughout 2026, even though the Tier I rate goes up every July. All providers, whether on Tier I or Tier II (and all providers not on the Food Program), will use the rates listed.

† Enter this amount on Form 1040 Schedule C, Part V. Be sure to enter any reimbursements from the Food Program (with the exception of reimbursements for your own children) as income on Form 1040 Schedule C, line 6.

EMERGENCY PHONE NUMBERS

PROVIDER'S ADDRESS		FIRE		POLICE	
		EMERGENCY SQUAD		POISON CONTROL CENTER	
PROVIDER'S PHONE #		LOCAL HOSPITAL		OTHER	

IN EMERGENCIES USE 911 IF AVAILABLE

Child's Name	Birth Date	Parent / Guardian		Parent / Guardian		Emergency Contact		Doctor	
		Name / Home #	Work # / Cell #	Name / Home #	Work # / Cell #	Name	Phone #	Name	Phone #

EMERGENCY PHONE NUMBERS (continued from page 96)

Child's Name	Birth Date	Parent / Guardian		Parent / Guardian		Emergency Contact		Doctor	
		Name / Home #	Work # / Cell #	Name / Home #	Work # / Cell #	Name	Phone #	Name	Phone #
		___	___	___	___	___	___	___	___
		___	___	___	___	___	___	___	___
		___	___	___	___	___	___	___	___
		___	___	___	___	___	___	___	___
		___	___	___	___	___	___	___	___
		___	___	___	___	___	___	___	___
		___	___	___	___	___	___	___	___
		___	___	___	___	___	___	___	___

Professional Development Courses and Hours

Date of Training	Title	Trainer	Level	Contact Hours	CEUs	Competency Area

WAITING LIST

Child's Name	Age	Parent/Guardian Names	Phone #	Date of Call	Date Needed
			W H W H		
			W H W H		
			W H W H		
			W H W H		
			W H W H		
			W H W H		
			W H W H		
			W H W H		
			W H W H		

EMERGENCY DRILL RECORD

	Time/Date	No. and Ages of Children	Type of Drill	Evac. Time
JAN			Fire	
FEB			Fire	
MAR			Fire	
APR			Fire	
MAY			Fire	
JUN			Fire	
JUL			Fire	
AUG			Fire	
SEP			Fire	
OCT			Fire	
NOV			Fire	
DEC			Fire	